A Flight of Fancy!

A collection of writings from

'The Big 40 Blog'

Margaret Henderson Smith

Published 2010 by arima publishing

www.arimapublishing.com

ISBN 978 1 84549 418 6

Printed and bound in the United Kingdom

Typeset in Garamond 12/16

Swirl is an imprint of arima publishing.

arima publishing
ASK House, Northgate Avenue
Bury St Edmunds, Suffolk IP32 6BB
t: (+44) 01284 700321

www.arimapublishing.com

Author's Note

Whilst this compilation of events is true, some have been drawn from memory and have been reconstructed here as accurately as I can recall. There may, therefore, be the inevitable errors and omissions in the detail. In the event, the reader can be assured the true spirit of the work remains unaffected.

Also by Margaret Henderson Smith
A Question of Answers
Ne Obliviscaris

www.margarethendersonsmith.co.uk

With love and thanks to

John

And all my dear family for making it possible

Never forgetting
Mum
&
Dad
&
His ever inspirational
Spirit of Thurso

Contents

About Margaret   9

It could so easily have been Harriet!   13

I don't believe it!   17

I surrender!   21

The very idea!   23

If only!   25

Sorry wrong place!   29

Men don't do The Big 40!   33

Spooky!   37

Not quite as expected!   41

Way over the top!   47

Oh no!   53

It usually happens that way!   61

No most definitely not!   69

No question about it!   75

Golly gosh!   81

No! I just can't go with that!   89

Too clever by half!   97

In trouble again!   109

I've got it all wrong again!   117

A kiss and a promise!   125

Down with a bump!   135

No thanks!   139

Reflections   147

About Margaret

I couldn't get it together at school. Just wasn't my bag at all.

Art? Project for the weekend. Still life. Went home. Painted the iron. Came back Monday. Teacher: "Looks like a grey jelly. Did you not consider a bowl of fruit?"

Domestic science? No better. Couldn't light the gas. Always bagged the electric cooker. Not the prized Rayburn. An altar for the tea towels. Piping hot on the top though. Told to dry the teacher's prize clear plastic storage jars. She nodded at it. 'Good place,' I thought. She asked for them. At four o'clock. Metamorphosed. All twisted, dripping long threads of hot melted plastic. Furious! She made me pay.

Custard? Always last! Waiting for the milk to boil. The rest of them. Going home. Missed the bus whilst my milk was frothing away. Rising angrily in volcanic mode before exploding. Laying the white enamel top of the cooker with a hot brown skin. Underneath. Milk everywhere! Regularly at four o'clock. Every time. Me! Back the next morning. Early bus. Cleaning the cooker to the silence of an empty school.

P.E? useless. Class teacher: "Margaret, why are you always absent on a Thursday?"

I wised up! Cleaning the cooker and P.E? Where was she coming from?

Time to leave school. Interviews. Decided to be a secretary. "Copy type this." She came back for it ten minutes later. Blank paper. Still hadn't worked out how to unlock the machine.

Scrutinised again! Serious business man. Looking for

competence. 'I really wanted to teach,' I told him. Interview immediately curtailed.

My anxious parents. Sent me off to make very posh raincoats. To be a machinist in Liverpool. Interview. They sat me down. Sample fabric. "Here. Stitch this," she said. Then came back. The machine still rattling. Wouldn't stop. Couldn't turn it off. Fabric trailed the floor strung to miles of twisted cotton. Ended up eating cakes in Reeces'.

Last resort. Very high class lingerie shop. Local. Just a bus ride away. Interview. Threw my 'O' levels at him. Got the job! Relief! Liked the bus conductors! Best part waving at them from the shop window whilst collecting up all the busts and bodies. Awkward things. Had to undress them. Kept falling out of the narrow cupboard as I struggled to pack them away for the weekend. All rigid. Uncooperative! Kept getting caught in the sliding doors. Every time! Kept missing my bus home.

'Had enough of this,' I told him. "You've got 'O' levels," he said. "I'll have a word with the Bank Manager next door." 'I really wanted to teach,' I replied. He didn't bother.

Parents. Now desperate. "Library. Try the library." Very nice Chief Librarian. Got the job. Finally started my working career surrounded in books. Fascinating! Especially when given the opportunity to buy them! I recall well, as the junior of a small group, the train trip up north. Being met at the station by this impressive bloke in his sumptuous car. Off to 'Holt Jackson' to fill our shopping trolleys with books. Free to select anything and everything at will. What a day! If only someone would throw mine into the basket. I'm working on it!

Then I met my sea-going engineer, John. For me, he swapped all that to learn the art of making huge propellers and rose rapidly to hold various managerial positions in the company. Two baby chicks in our nest. Two beautiful daughters. Left the library. Did an honours degree with the Open University as I watched them grow. Went on to a teacher training college in Liverpool for a year to gain a Certificate in Education. Taught for a few years then wanted to do my own thing. Coupled supply teaching with running my own private pre-school. Then my dear Mum departed from the material world to the intangible. Sorting her care motivated me to establish my own care and service agency. Interesting work. Often matching the very well to do with those of us who meet their needs.

Daughters grew. Met two great lads. Brothers! Now we have four beautiful grandchildren. We help out in between walking, sailing, camping, gardening, reading. And now writing. Which brings me full circle.

Thanks to arima I've also discovered the joys of blogging. It may take a while but eventually, through this medium I'm hoping to get to know you. Hoping to get to know my readers. Hoping my readers will get to know me. Hoping you'll visit www.margarethendersonsmith.co.uk and leave a few lines. I'm hoping after reading this you'll share your everyday happenings.

In the meantime because words have always sat comfortably with paper and are much too precious to be left floating in cyberspace, I've decided to make it a little easier for those who can't or don't particularly want to log on. Sometimes, if we've enjoyed reading a book we're not quite ready to let go of it. So whilst waiting for the next, what could be better than discovering a little about the author? What could be better for the author than her readers wanting to know the source of inspiration for the story? So this is for you. For you because you love the feel of a book. For you because you want to read it unhindered, in your own time, without reaching for a switch. For you because you might want to pass it along, or just keep it. For you with my thanks for choosing to take 'A Flight of Fancy!' with me.

It could so easily have been Harriet!

So I've finally managed to dip my toes into this unbelievably scary world of blogging. Why bother? You might ask. Well it's mostly because I want to get to know my readers. People who enjoyed the book enough to want to ask questions or discuss the issues raised. I'd love to hear from anyone out there who feels they can identify with any of the characters/situations in the story. It's your experiences, opinions, ideas that are going to make this blog interesting.

We're talking about everyday life here, exactly where my stories are rooted. From the exciting to the mundane, the polarities of which are so subjective I hesitate to describe it as a continuum; however, wherever we are on it at any given point in time, there is always something of interest to be had, always something to learn, something to better understand from others.

Where to start? How about a few lines about what pleased, disappointed, frustrated, delighted, or annoyed you today, yesterday, last week, last month, or last year? Start wherever you wish and once you have finished consider whether you can attribute anything of what you write to The Big 40, whether you are anticipating it, in it, or long past it. Without identifying people or places let's generalise our experiences and share them for all to enjoy.

For instance I'll start the ball rolling with this piece of trivia.

A little less than two weeks ago I was permanently online in pursuit of a 'Brand New With Tags' designer pure silk blouse.

Absolutely gorgeous! I watched it, bid on it and to my absolute delight, won it! Desperate to wear it I had it in and out of the drawer until finally it settled on top of one of the large black suitcases cluttering the house, together with boxes and bags of stuff just waiting to go camping.

'I don't believe it! You're not taking that with you?' came my husband's incredulous tones.

'Haven't decided yet,' I replied, knowing full well he was right.

The phone rings.

'Estate agent,' I say. 'Viewers. Sold theirs, they want to come as soon as possible.'

'I don't believe it!' My better half again.

The 'For Sale' board is just that. Bored! Tilting in disinterest having been virtually ignored for nearly two years. Like the one down the road. They drop the price, we drop the price and so it goes on.

It had to be done of course, but not quite at this moment. I look out of the window. Suddenly I see the car and the camper groaning under the weight.

'I don't believe it! We're taking even more than last time.'

I pretend I haven't heard as I scurry round trying to make the house fit for viewers. They arrive. It looks like a show house. They like it.

'It was worth it,' I say.

A quick call from the estate agent before we go.

'They're interested in another viewing,' I'm told.

In a rush of joy I sneak to the car to put my silk blouse in the case.

'I don't believe it!' Exasperation from over my shoulder. I pretend not to hear.

Good week camping, though, spending odd moments dreaming about a new house.

On the way back about five miles from home we meet with a huge black cloud.

'I don't believe it!' comes the familiar refrain.

We follow it all the way to the front gate. Then something akin to a tropical rain storm descends. The camper tyres skidding as we try to push the huge lump of virtual house onto the drive. I feel bad. I wanted this upgrade. I close my ears. My better half's polite refrain now changed to something distinctly unprintable. Suddenly an extra pair of hands. A very good neighbour.

'I believe the house down the road's been sold,' he says.

'I don't believe it,' I think as I overload the washing machine. A couple of hours later I'm still thinking as I pull the massive ball of hot, dry washing from the tumble dryer. My heart sinks even further. My new silk blouse. I tug away as it refuses to relinquish itself from the tangle. I hold it up. It's shrunk!

'I don't believe it!' I think. I try it on. My husband says it looks much better now. I don't think so. I wish I'd listened to him in the first place!

It could so easily have been 'Harriet'. She would most definitely have put it down to The Big 40. Me? I'm not so sure. I've always had a precarious relationship with the washing machine, but that's another story for another time. If I must switch something on then let it be the computer. Writing over washing any day!

And so it's over to you, I hope. Or me, once I've de-shrunk the blouse and de-bored the board and figured out the answers to any other of life's impossible questions.

I don't believe it!

Still with the holiday theme, a few years back we had a lovely family break in Devon. We went to Hope Cove, a magical place and stayed in a delightful hotel overlooking the sea. It was a perfect holiday, it's just that the rub is generally in the home-coming.

'Where's my diamond pendant?' I ask as I'm returning the rest of my jewellery to its box.

'Oh no, I don't believe it!' comes my better-half's familiar refrain. 'You haven't left it in the hotel, have you?'

'I think so,' I say. I feel sad. It was a very special Christmas present from him. We search and search but no luck. I'm promised another.

Still missing and a few weeks before Christmas I decide to go online. I spend many happy hours searching but as you'd expect, diamonds bid up. They go very high. I start scrolling the lab creations. It doesn't feel right. I go back to the diamonds and unbelievably I spot one, "As new, hardly worn, Bid or Buy it Now". I consult my better-half and 'buy it now'.

'You can't have it until Christmas,' he says.

I can't wait for Christmas to come to wear it, though I live with the niggling thought of why someone should have wanted to sell it. I try to put it from my mind.

'That's not your concern, it's merely a business transaction.' Wise words from my husband.

Christmas comes and goes. I finally give up looking for the old one but my ethical concerns about the new one refuse to go away.

I notice the clasp starting to stick but I keep wearing it. The other day in the car as my husband backs off the drive, I go to touch the diamond. It's not there! Undone, the fallen chain loops into my blouse. I can't find the diamond anywhere. I spend the next few days searching, searching for them both. Finally I rummage in the top drawer of the dressing table at the back where I keep a few old bracelet boxes. I take one and open the lid. Just as expected it's empty. I go to close the box then suddenly decide to lift the black velvet liner. There, underneath, is the original diamond pendant. It's a complete mystery! I'm ecstatic. I simply don't believe it!

Today we are backing off the drive. Head down I'm yet again rummaging around wondering if my 'unethical' diamond has gone down the side of the seat after all. I look up.

'I don't believe it,' I say. 'The board's gone!' The bored board has totally vanished. Unbelievable in the face of my first post. Once back we inspect the spot. No obvious signs of removal. No footprints in the springy lawn, no spread of soil, just a small hole in the ground and nothing else.

I phone the estate agent. They know nothing of it. They are wondering, too. How can a 'For Sale' board vanish without sight nor sound?

And so to the other question in my mind.

How could it be the first diamond pendant judiciously appeared at the right moment?

Could I have sensed a sad history to the one I lost? Was I never meant to have it? It never really felt mine.

I've taken to wearing Harriet's 'Faith, Hope and Charity'

pendant just now. I feel comfortable with it as I think of the lost diamond and someone's need to sell it. Like the 'For Sale' board, I wish somehow it could make its way back to where it belongs.

And in case you are wondering, none of this would ever have crossed my mind before The Big 40. I'm not sure if that's a good or bad thing. You decide!

I surrender!

I open the door to my three rosy apples and their mummy. Their eyes wide, I see computers in them. In silent reluctance I surrender. Today I know it's not my turn. They rush past to stampede their way up the stairs, tripping as they go. There are three up there, but it's not either of the old ones they're interested in. It's mine! Mine's the new one and they stick to it like bees in a honeypot. If it's not 'Pokemon' or 'PollyPocket', very soon it's going to be 'Moshi Monsters' filling the screen.

I say 'very soon' because a couple of days ago I look over her shoulder to see a registration form. She's three. She points to the three green ticks. She's put her name in, something else and the password.

'I've done that right,' she says, 'Now you do your email in there.'

'Help!' I think, 'She's better at it than me!'

Back to today. I watch her judge it as the scramble upstairs suddenly goes quiet. Still on the bottom stair. Her long dark lashes fringe the determination in her ever widening eyes.

'I'm going on the old one,' she announces.

'That's good,' I say, thankful she's not desperate to be online. That one was never connected. 'Lots of games to play on that.' I try to sound convincing. All's quiet. I follow her upstairs. She glides onto the empty chair clicking her way into 'Polly Pocket'.

'I thought you wanted to go on this one to play games,' I say, anticipating the worst.

'No! This old one!' she replies. Suddenly it breaks! World War III!

'I wanted that one!' My middle apple wails.

'Why didn't you go on it then?' I ask.

'Because I wanted that one!' She points to mine.

Now completely transmogrified my biggest apple refuses to budge from her Pokemon world. The little one keeps her head down. Her strategy has paid off!

Suddenly, the slam of a car door.

'Oh look out there,' I say. 'I think that man's bringing us a new 'For Sale Board.'

I watch him stand on the wall as he hammers away at the post, driving it hard into the ground. He picks up the board, looks at it then takes it back to the boot of his car. I wonder why? He fishes out another. Holds it up. A band of bright red sits across the top. 'SALE AGREED' it says. My heart sinks as I feel the intensity of disappointment returning.' What is this man trying to do to me?'

Then I watch him unbutton the red band. He drives away. Back to the boring board.

'I want to go on that computer!' The wail regenerates.

'What about playing some games on this one?' I suggest.

'That's boring,' she replies.

'You and me both,' I say as I glance at the fully requisitioned screens and then out at the newly planted board. 'Come on let's go and say goodbye to mummy.'

She pulls me down the stairs then lets my hand go so she can jump the last one. She's happy again. It's infectious!

Grandchildren? A totally unexpected bonus after The Big 40!

The very idea!

It's bin day. Garden bin day to be precise. I follow my better-half out, collecting the trail of fallen branch cuttings as he pushes the conifer-laden bin to the front. I look up. It's that big black cloud again threatening to break into another of those tropical rain storms. He's pleased he's got that job out of the way.

'Just in time I think,' he says.

It's early morning and busy out there. Suddenly, right opposite where there's never been a bus-stop we see a double-decker pull in. It brakes to a halt. The engine's ticking over. We are being looked at! Every head behind every window turns to face us. The driver jumps out and leaps dangerously in and out of the traffic to reach us. He lands at our feet.

'I had to do it! I just had to do it! Every day I drive past here and today I said I'm doing it!'

My mind races.

'It's the house, he wants to buy it!' I think.

'No, no, it's the board. He witnessed the theft. It was dumped on his route. He wants to tell us!' My thoughts escalate.

'No, no, it's got to be the diamond. He's prised it from his tyre tread.'

I decide it's time to leave them. Time to return to Harriet as my thinking becomes excessively creative. I move to go.

'Want to sell it?' He points his finger at the camper. 'They're good these. We had one just like that but it got pinched a couple of weeks ago.'

I feel the first drops of rain as I look across to the waiting passengers. My husband scratches his head, looks at the tyres, the path, then back to the camper covering rapidly in large wet spots. I know exactly what he's thinking! I wonder if he's going to seize the opportunity to go back to less tonnage. He turns to me.

'Fancy a tent?' He asks, laughing.

I have no need to reply.

He shakes his head at the bus-driver, 'Not this time anyway but thanks for asking.'

'Oh well you've got to try!' comes the good-natured response.

He shoots back to his bus. I shoot back to my computer.

'A tent? Never! The very idea!'

That's definitely one thing The Big 40 hasn't changed!

If only!

I look forward to seeing my rosy apples on the doorstep, but in the fleeting second they face me, I see today one of them's turned green. I feel the draught as they thunder up the stairs, landing on top of one another in a screeching heap.

'Come back,' says my biggest apple's mummy. 'You're supposed to be ill.'

Down she comes to be ill. She lies on the sofa as I switch her favourite TV programme on. I return to the others. I see little apple has done well having abandoned her former strategy. She's already logged on to my computer. I am thankful middle apple seems OK with the old one today. In unison they give Polly Pocket pink hair and a matching guitar. They both up the volume. The house pulsates. 'At this rate they'll hit 'The Big 40' before they even get to be teenagers,' I think as I go downstairs. I look at my watch. Soon it will be school and playgroup's turn. I let them enjoy it.

They go. All is quiet.

I cover my big apple with a quilt and tell her I'll be upstairs on the computer if she needs me. I feel bad. It's not my day. I decide to dust it instead. Before I know it I've dusted everything. I'm moving from room to room, save that where my green apple is. I go in.

'Where is she?' I ask my better-half.

'Three guesses,' he laughs.

It's lunch time. My better-half goes to bring little apple home. I go in search of big apple.

'Are you feeling better?' I ask.

'Only a bit,' she says, swivelling her chair back towards my computer.

We both stare at the eager pair of hands carefully stripping away the wrapper from a gleaming new pack of Pokemon cards. She's transfixed by the narration. This is serious stuff!

'It's OK,' she says, anticipating my next question. 'Mummy says it's OK for me to watch these.'

'Shall I join you?'

She doesn't answer.

'Right, I won't disturb you then. I'll go downstairs.'

I find little apple happily playing the pirate game. I see my better-half's one gold coin. She's got six. She's winning!

'Can I join in?' I ask.

She shakes her head. I return to the duster. Finished, I look around. Empty vase, bereft of flowers. I look out of the front window. Roses! Before I know it I'm out doing battle with a clutch of thorny stems. I try to be inconspicuous, then 'Ouch!' A thorn the size of a dragon's tooth straight into my thumb! I look up.

'Your name Rowl….' A neighbour waves a letter at me. I'm in serious pain. I shake my head at him as I drop my hard won blooms.

'If only,' I think.

He nods towards the board. I shake my head again. He smiles and walks away.

'If only,' I think again. I go in.

Still sucking the pain from my thumb I coax my thorny

experience into the vase and plonk it by the hearth.

'Fit for a viewer,' I think. 'If only!'

The phone rings. 'Can you manage a viewing early tomorrow morning? He's in rented. Nothing to sell.' I don't believe it!

'Not again!' groans my better-half before going to collect middle apple.

They come back. She rushes upstairs to bag my computer. I ask if she's had a good day in school.

'I'm going to live in this house when I'm grown-up,' she suddenly says.

'And why would you want to do that?' I ask.

'Because everthing's nice,' she replies.

Smiling, I hug my middle apple. I think of greener grass. I think of the unattainable. I think of Harriet and her dreams. I wonder if life's experience beyond 'The Big 40' counts for anything. I wonder if the 'if only' factor ever goes away. Maybe you can tell me.

Sorry wrong place!

We wave goodbye to our viewer. He liked it a lot though he told us he still has a couple more to see. I'm convinced he'll go for it. His unmistakable enthusiasm inspires me. I'm surfing the net looking for the right house to buy. I see a bungalow, identical to the one we moved from. It's just a few doors away in the very same road. We needed to go. We'd over-done it a bit with the down-sizing, especially as more baby apples came along. I continue scrolling.

'No, we don't want another one of those,' I'm thinking. I missed the space. I missed my up-stairs.

There was something about it, though. Something that drew people to it. Let me explain. One light summer evening we are sitting in the lounge when suddenly a man's face appears at the side window, hard pressed against the glass. He starts banging and knocking and gesticulating. My husband goes out. He disappears for ages. Finally I see them both chatting on the drive. I'm filled with curiosity but stay put in the hope of enlightenment.

'Any minute now,' I think. I keep thinking. At last he comes in.

'He spotted the bikes,' my better-half finally informs me. I'm left wondering how four old motorbikes could possibly generate such unbridled enthusiasm.

It doesn't stop there, though. One day we return home to find a chap with a clipboard peering in through the front windows, moving from one to the other and then back again to the front door.

'What's he doing?' says my better-half as we drive in.

'Oh there you are,' the man says, 'there doesn't look too much wrong with this double glazing, actually. Still it's the conservatory we're looking at. You're thinking of a new one?'

'No. Not us thank you!' My husband is brief and to the point. No room for intervention there!

The man checks his clipboard. Checks the number on the door.

'Sorry! Wrong place!' he says. He scoots off.

I open the top front bedroom window. Later I return to see the postman fully stretched, pinned against the glass with his arm through the opening. A parcel lands on the bed!

'Sorry! Wrong place!' I think. He's away.

It's lunch time, I'm making sandwiches. I'm listening to one of those light-hearted radio programmes. Suddenly the door swings open. I jump! A complete stranger! He's standing in the kitchen. I don't believe it!

'As I'm in the area I just thought I'd pop in to see how Mrs. … is doing. I'm her doctor. Shall I go through?' he asks.

'Sorry! Wrong place!' I say. He disappears leaving a wake of profuse apologies.

I recall the bus driver and the camper. I wonder if this place is shaping up the same way. I continue scrolling. The phone rings.

'Yes he liked your house very much indeed,' the estate agent informs me. 'He's made appointments to see two more this week, then he's going to make his decision.'

I put the phone down. I tell my better-half I think he's going to buy it. We start looking, just in case.

'Let's drive past the one advertised in the paper. The one that's just come on the market,' my husband suggests.

'But it's a bungalow,' I protest. 'Just because you get past The Big 40 doesn't mean to say you've got to live in a little bungalow. You tried that one last time. Sorry! Wrong place!'

He laughs as he drives me straight past the road.

Men don't do The Big 40!

Yesterday big apple had her birthday party. Well I say 'her' birthday party with some reservation. The kids all disappeared upstairs. We had a whale of a time. The men were in good form. It was bouncing off the four of them. From one to the other like a game of doubles. We girls of course, took it all in our stride. On such occasions we're used to it, side swipes from the men. Nevertheless, I'm admiring them all. Thinking how like red wine all men are with age always on their side.

'No "Big 40?" issues with them,' I think.

We laugh ourselves silly to the sound of wine bottles slooshing themselves empty. Even the dog wants to join in, obliterating the sea view as she jumps up and down on the trampoline outside, trying to look through the window. It becomes too much for this big brown chocolate Labrador. She gives up to perch on the corner of the bench under the window, peering into the glass of red wine from the wrong side of the window sill.

'If only!' I almost hear her think.

'Mind the black bags,' I say to my scrambling apples as they thud up the stairs the next morning. I've been doing some sorting in anticipation of the move. Well, the motivation wasn't quite as clear cut as that. My better-half needed some stamps.

'In the back of my purse,' I say.

'This purse is as disorganised as your bag,' he shouts up the stairs.

'Huh!' I think. 'He's lucky to be allowed in there.'

'As disorganised as your office!' he finishes.

I take the hint. I start sorting and shredding before we go off to the party.

'It was good,' I think as we pile into the car to deliver our apples to where they go. I look at the board, any minute now the phone will ring. I just know he'll want a second viewing. I visualise the red 'sold' sign along the top as we drive past.

Our apples get safely distributed. On the way back I'm still smiling.

'What is it about the collective consciousness that makes us smile and keep smiling when we see someone famous?' I ask my better-half.

'Get a move on!' he replies to the little green and white car in front. 'You've passed your test haven't you?'

'That's exactly why she's put that green "P" plate on,' I try to explain, 'so people like you won't get annoyed!'

I'm still smiling. I would be. Someone I've only ever seen on TV has just smiled and said 'Good morning,' to us. He was most charming. Charmingly mature. Another bottle of red wine! I try to recall any other famous people we've seen. An MP in Birkenhead. A PM conducting the Liverpool Philharmonic Orchestra. The Queen looking radiant, waving from her car window, twice. I remember smiling at the teacher. I remember smiling at my pupils. Oh yes, and another MP, a cabinet member at the time kindly held the door open for my husband once when he was on business in London. And that's about it really. No wonder I'm smiling.

We return home.

'Right,' says my husband as he eyes the full to bursting bin-bags on the landing. 'Which of these have got to go and which still need shredding?'

I pull the one sitting by the door back into the office.

'I'll do that when we get back,' I say. 'It can go with the rest of it after lunch.'

We go. He drives straight to the right skip and tips it all in. It's windy, I see it starting to blow around.

It's that big black cloud again. We follow it back. It looks like rain. I switch the shredder on and reach for an assortment of identifiable paper from the black bag. I don't believe it! Wrong one! I start shredding innocuous stuff in the hope my better-half won't notice. I shudder at the thought of all that lost confidentiality being blown on the wind. I look at the sky. I want it to rain. I want the contents of the skip to turn to papier-mache.

Caught in fear, I'm still shredding needlessly while my better-half goes to bring little apple back. Finally I tie the bag and put it with the rest.

After lunch we're on our way back with the rest of the bags. I hope he won't notice. He finds the same skip, empties them all, then looks down. Foot-marked receipts, mini bank-statements, anything and everything that escaped the shredder blowing around. Impossible to catch.

'I hope they're not ours,' he says as he gets back into the car.

He sees my face.

'They are, aren't they?'

'Could be anybody's,' I hedge.

'Anyway, fancy seeing him this morning. What a surprise. You know I was watching you all at the party. All of you men. How is it that men just get better with age? I bet "The Big 40?" never even crosses your minds.'

He suddenly smiles. It starts to rain. I'm happy again. For the moment at least I've kept the cork from popping on my bottle of red wine! I just want the phone to ring now.

Spooky!

Today, no apples. I have a whole day to spend with my computer whilst my better-half is busy grouting the tiles in his newly completed utility. His talents are diverse and many. Knowledge flows from him like wine, only my bottle of red never depletes. His brilliance is second to none. I leave him to it.

I'm back with Harriet, time's moving on. I'm thinking about the estate agent. 'Any minute now, there'll be a call.'

The doorbell goes. I go down to answer it. No one there! I return to my computer. It goes again, and again, and again. I go down. Still no one there. Puzzled, I return to my work.

'Spooky, not Halloween yet,' I think.

The phone goes. It's the estate agent.

'I've just had an unusual call. Someone wants to buy it,' she says. 'She saw it on the internet and wants it.'

'Without a viewing?' I gasp.

I take the offer to my better-half.

'Tell them we'll stick that one to the wall for the time being.'

I'm disappointed. I return to my work. Back to Harriet. The doorbell goes again. I shoot downstairs. Still no one there. Even spookier! I look for my better-half to tell him. Nowhere to be seen.

Back to my computer again. All manner of spooky thoughts suddenly come to mind. I think of that very old hotel in the Devon countryside. The one where the owner behind the bar tells me our room is haunted. He speaks of a long lost soul who'd had his life grotesquely taken. He sets the historical scene.

All this just before we are about to turn in for the night. I don't believe it! I want us to stay just where we are.

'Don't be so silly,' says my knowledgeable better-half.

We go upstairs. Everything creaks. I shiver. I don't want to be there.

'He's talking it up. Good for the trade!'

Without success my husband tries to reassure me. All night I cling to him, banking on his faultless knowledge. All night I think, 'Never again!'

And never again it was! I'm speaking of a last minute family gathering. We needed a hotel.

'Just one room left,' the manager says. 'It's beautiful, the bridal suite. All on its own right on the very top floor.'

'Hang on a minute,' I think. 'The bridal suite? A bit late for that. Almost a child bride, me. Long before The Big 40! No, I'd feel silly in there!'

'Do you wish to book it?' he's asking on the other end of the phone.

I think quickly. I go for it. At least it's not haunted!

We arrive. Endless flights of dark narrow stairs take us to our room. We meet the door. It's shaped like a coffin. We go in, ducking under the thick, heavy, dark wooden beams hanging low from the ceiling. All around looking like sets of gallows.

'It's spooky,' I declare. My better-half despairs.

I phone my littlest apple's mummy. 'Can't stay here. We're going to have to find something else.' I feel bad. I disrupt all the arrangements. One of our kindly couples swap. They're up for an adventure. I'll always be grateful.

Back to today. I suddenly remember, we're going to see littlest apple and his mummy and daddy soon. I need to book the hotel. Relief! Availability. I book it. I'm OK with this one. It's the other end of town.

I'm deviating. I get back to my work. It's the phone again.

'The gentleman that came last week. He wants a second viewing.' I'm delighted. I tell my better half.

'We need to find a house,' I think. 'He might just want to buy it. Not anything spooky though.'

Not like the one we used to live in. Well, there wasn't enough to positively identify it as such, but there were some unexplainables.

One day, I'm sewing. My better half's at work. The children are at school. I'm by myself. I stop sewing. All's quiet. Then suddenly the machine takes off and starts rattling away, all on its own! Spooked, I regress to little apple status, jump in the car and decide to go shopping. I stop sewing after that.

And there was the evening we were all together. The conversation turns to spooks. I recall my sewing machine story. It widens out. We're all laughing nervously as spooky tales come to light. Suddenly a loud explosion. Then silence!

We look at one another while my better half investigates. He's looking in the kitchen cupboard. Glass everywhere, shattered into hundreds of tiny pieces. Everything swimming in sticky, undiluted orange squash.

'Spooky,' we all say.

Back to today, again. I'm making little progress. The doorbell goes again. This time I try to find my better half. He suddenly appears. I go running towards him then trip, straight into his arms.

I think of Harriet. He laughs and points to the vacuum cleaner.

'How could you possibly miss that? It's like a big orange pumpkin!'

I think of Halloween. I think of spooks.

'Someone's been ringing our doorbell,' I say.

'Why didn't you answer it, then?' His face is straight.

'By the time I get there, they've gone.' I insist.

'Gone?'

'Yes gone. No sign of anyone.'

'It might have been either or both the viewers. Couldn't wait for an appointment. Look what you've missed!' He's laughing. 'You don't change much, do you?' he says.

I think of The Big 40. I think of all things spooky. I think it's made no difference. I think there's no correlation between maturity and the rationalisation of fear, though it's open to debate, of course.

I turn to my better half.

'Someone has most definitely been ringing the doorbell,' I insist.

'It was me. I've been fixing it,' he laughs. 'You wouldn't want viewers left floundering on the doorstep, now would you?'

There's just no answer to my clever bottle of red!

Not quite as expected!

He arrives. It's his second viewing. We recede. We remain as inconspicuous as possible to allow him complete freedom of the house. He is asking all the right questions. His smile is unmistakable. I think he will buy it. We are merely waiting for the call.

The phone rings. It's the estate agent.

'It's the lady who saw it on the internet again. She'd like to arrange a viewing. They are most anxious to see it.'

We arrange a viewing. They come. They ask all the right questions.

'Got to be a better offer this time,' I think.

I'm excited. 'We'd better start looking, too,' I suggest to my better-half. 'Any day now it will all come together.'

I trawl online for possibilities. I'm trying to work out garden sizes. Suddenly my better-half is over my shoulder.

'That's not much good,' he says. 'Try Google earth.'

Before I know it I'm looking at a map of Europe. It looks very familiar. Tiny red dots set everywhere against the green terrain, marking out towns, cities. As he zooms in this familiar sight suddenly becomes very significant.

'Stop!' I say. 'Please stop just there. Zoom out a minute.'

'It's back gardens we're trying to get to. We're not looking at buying the best part of Europe!'

'No, no,' I say. 'It's the map. I've seen it before. It looks just like the map on my social site.'

'Social site?' he queries.

'Yes social site. Remember, I told you about it? As soon as I became a member I told you about all the red dots, all the places all over the world where people have clicked on my site to see my book. Do you remember how I couldn't believe the huge response?'

'Vaguely,' he says. I see that 'Oh no not again' expression on his face.

'Well,' I say. 'Why do some of those red dots exactly match the red dots on my social site home page?'

'Probably because places tend not to move around.' He laughs. 'You haven't quite got the hang of it yet, have you?'

'No,' I say. 'Not quite as expected!'

He leaves me to my bitter disappointment. The similarity of the maps. I've got to have misinterpreted all that data. I'm wondering just how can I manage to loose a whole world full of interest in one swipe? I was only looking for a back garden!

I continue to zoom in as I marvel at this modern miracle. I hadn't quite realised all these virtual trips down virtual roads, all this route planning, had emerged from a world map covered in little red dots. 'No wonder they haven't turned green yet,' I think. 'No wonder they haven't shed their anonymity.

I am reminded we're going away. Heading south to see littlest apple. Well worn route this one. No need to play, I've got work to be getting on with. Once I've logged onto my favourite auction, that is. My favourite place to be. I need a new jacket, for the trip. I absolutely refuse to wear mine any more. I won that one, too. 'Brand New With Tags' and exactly what I was looking for, at the time. I was pleased with my pale pink bargain, until I saw it walking around. Everywhere! Until people started saying. 'I thought it was you for a minute. From the back.'

I think of the collective consciousness. I think how readily we can lose our identity in droves for the famous. I think how little we like our identity being taken away on the street.

'Not quite as expected,' I think.

Back to the trip. Well we may not get there yet. The car's decided to play up just as we're about to go away. It usually happens.

'We've got to be thinking about replacing it,' my better-half informs me.

'I'll sell it for you.' I offer.

'No you will not!' He declares.

'You mean the "silver slipper",' I say.

'Exactly!'

It felt like the most sumptuous car in the world. So it was christened. Alas, its life was limited. On the day we part company my better-half leaves a list of faults.

'Make sure he reads this,' he says. 'It's only worth… Now don't be trying to get more.'

My better-half goes to work. I collude with my chicks.

'But its worth far more than that. It's luxuriously comfortable and it looks good,' we decide.

The doorbell goes. The fault list goes straight out of my head.

'Sold as seen.' At least I remember to say that. He looks it over. He agrees.

He drives it away. We've talked up the price. We can't wait to spill the good news.

Good news? No most definitely not, I've never seen my better-half so cross. I look at my chicks in silence. The phone goes. He's taken it to the garage. Had it checked out. He's bringing it back. We return his money. I hide in the back as I hear my husband apologising profusely. I feel bad. He closes the door.

'I'm not suprised it was "Not quite as expected," he storms. 'Don't you ever do that again. Well you won't get the chance!'

Back to today. I must break from my work. We've got a viewing. We go to see a house not too far away.

'Oh look,' says my better-half. 'There's your pink jacket again.'

'Actually I've disowned it.'

He laughs as we drive up to the smartly dressed girl with a clipboard, standing on the drive. It needs work, more work than we thought.

'No. Definitely not,' declares my better-half. 'Not quite as expected!'

We drive away. Every time we brake the car clanks. We come home. I look out of the window. Suddenly the grass looks greener! I go to the front. Already my clever better-half has the wheels off.

'I need some more rags,' he says, as I look at his oily hands.

I run in. I run out with my pink jacket. 'Here use this before it goes in the bin.'

I hear the phone. It's the estate agent. They've made an offer. We turn it down.

'Not quite as expected!' I think. I'm disappointed. I'm trying to think cheerful. I think of my book. There's always a chance of a significant red spot appearing somewhere in the world. It might even turn green! I check it out. I think I should have been looking for little red and green balloons. 'Not quite as expected!' I return to my writing. I return to Harriet. I think of The Big 40.

'Now that definitely was "Not quite as expected!" No disappointment there!'

Way over the top!

We are busy getting ready for our trip. The phone rings. It's the estate agent again.

'HIP, they want to see the HIP. They might increase the offer. We don't appear to have a copy. Have you got one?'

'We've got it on disc,' I reply, racking my brains trying to recall if we were ever sent a written one.

I turn on the computer. I need to email the question to the HIP surveyor.

'It's a straightforward question. Keep it short and to the point!' I hear my better-half being bossy over my shoulder.

'You know what I'm like with emails,' I protest. 'I find it very difficult keeping to the point. Anyway he was a nice chatty guy. There's nothing wrong with sending a friendly one.'

He shakes his head in exasperation. 'Way over the top!'

'Come here,' he says. 'I'll do it!'

I watch him type two lines as if there's a tax on words.

'Now that's the way it should be done.'

I try to take it onboard. I think about writing. I think about writing for fun. I think about how difficult it is to turn it all off.

He lets me have my computer back. I need a jacket. I go to my favourite auction again. I am greeted with words. "Feed your passion for Pokemon."

'No thank you,' I decide. I really don't have a passion for Pokemon. Now if they'd said "writing", I'd be more than happy to go along with it. I show my better-half.

'Just an example of over the top writing,' I suggest. He laughs. 'It's still not as bad as the stuff you come out with. You couldn't even compile a straightforward road-sign!'

I am reminded we are going away. We need to leave the keys with our nearest and dearest as my rosy apples and their mummy and daddy are on holiday. According to big apple they've all flown to a 'tropical island'. I make the phone call.

'If you wouldn't mind just collecting the post, please.'

I think about letters, cards. The written word in all manner and form. I need to write birthday cards before we go. Again the voice of my wise-one from behind.

'Happy Birthday will do. Just keep it simple. No need to write "War and Peace". Oh no! You're not writing two for each of them again, are you? Way over the top!'

I protest. One card for the occasion, one for the present. I can't see anything wrong. I think of wrong writing as my better-half leaves me to it. I recall my experience as press officer to the local community association some time ago. I'm delighted with my recent appointment. I can't wait to tell the local newspaper all about the new building. I am writing my piece as honestly as I can. I open the evening paper. A headline, "New Community Centre Nobody Wants." I die a thousand deaths. I apologise and resign my post. No comfort from my better-half. 'That's you,' he says. 'Way over the top!'

Back to today. I'm not having any luck with my jacket so we go to the shops. We are looking at toys, trying to find something to take to littlest apple. All of a sudden a voice from behind us.

'What are you doing here? You're not welcome here! You're not welcome here looking like that. Go away you don't belong here.'

I jump. 'But that's exactly why I've come. For a new jacket,' I think. We turn round. No one to be seen. My better-half laughs as it starts all over again. We look at the toys round and about. All boxed.

'Of course it's coming from one of these,' he says.

'Huh! Fine way to get business. Way over the top!' I reply. We choose a big red racing car for littlest apple and I find a jacket.

All set to go. Our nearest and dearest call in to collect the keys. We sit in a foursome for a few minutes drinking tea.

'Did you see him on television last night?' I'm asked.

'I did,' I reply, beaming to the sound of the men groaning. We talk about politics. A few heated moments debating our pet dislikes.

'Now,' I say, if he were Prime Minister he'd do something about all of it. He's the personification of common sense.'

'Never!' groan the men. 'He's way over the top!'

'Oh no he isn't,' I reply, 'just wait and see. One day he'll be leader of his party. One day he'll be PM. One day he'll be delighting the nation.' They laugh. I'm serious.

At last we're on our way. I think of our conversation of yesterday afternoon. I think of this one famous person I would really like to meet. I think of his books, his writing, his intelligence, his wit. I am less than miniscule. He is grander than grand. I want to write. I want to leave feedback for his book. I want to pluck up the courage. Alas, I decide I am not worthy.

We are motoring. Mile after mile. We join the motorway, the road signs are starting to appear for London. The numbers are getting smaller.

'There, that's how to write a road sign,' my husband laughs, observing my intense interest in them.

'We're only sixty four miles away from him,' I inform my better-half.

'Sixty four miles away from who?' he asks.

'Sixty four miles away from our future Prime Minister,' I say. He laughs as we turn off the motorway. We join the A34. Road works on the other side. 'Must find a different way back,' my better-half suggests. I look at the map. We join the M4. Those signs for London again.

'We're only forty four miles from our future PM now,' I say. He laughs again.

'Oh no you're not. Don't forget he's in Manchester at the moment. You're getting further and further away from him by the minute!' I pretend I haven't heard.

'How about we go back via London?'

'Most definitely not!' declares my husband. 'That's way over the top!'

We arrive. From under his mop of blonde hair littlest apple smiles with those big blue eyes. He loves his red car. We leave him with his mummy and daddy as we make our way to the hotel. It's fine this one. We've stayed here before. Not on the top floor though. Not in the attic. We wind our way up two flights of stairs. The floors are uneven. It feels like we're at sea. The window's too high to see out of. I try to sink that spooky feeling. I turn the television on. It keeps going off. Turning itself off for no reason at all. I look at my better-half.

'Sorry, wrong place,' I say.

'Nothing at all wrong with it,' he declares. 'A silly reaction. Way over the top!'

I try to believe him. Most of our time will be spent with littlest apple and his mummy and daddy. I settle down. Dining is superb. We are having a lovely time.

Today we are all taking a drive in the countryside. We come across a new housing development. We love show houses littlest apple's mummy and I. We nod our heads in agreement. Next thing we're all inside. Interior designed to perfection, even the jars of preserves on the kitchen side blend in with the decor. Littlest apple's busy rearranging the black and red sports cars sitting on the designer bedroom window sill. We hear the men debating the lack of doors.

'Way over the top,' declares my better-half on the way out. 'Don't be getting any ideas!'

'If only!' I think.

We are on our way home. I think about writing. I've got work to do when we get back. No black cloud leading the way this time. We drive the whole way watching the sun from a clear blue sky painting all the shades of autumn into the countryside. A perfect day to end a perfect break.

We drive in.

'Oh look, we've got a new board,' declares my observant better-half.

'It looks the same to me,' I reply.

'Different phone number. They've opened a branch in the village remember?'

I can't wait to go in. There may be a message. Yes! A message!

We play it. It's them. It's the estate agent. I'm excited as I anticipate almost the asking price.

'Mr. and Mrs… are still thinking about it. We'll let you know if we hear any more.'

'Oh!' I say.

My better-half moves to the pile of post. He's holding a hand-written note.

'Oh look! There's one here asking if we want to sell the boat.'

'First the camper, now the boat. Why can't we get one about buying the house?' I can't conceal my disappointment.

'Stop whinging,' demands my better-half. He shows me the note. 'Look, that's how to write them. Short and to the point.'

'Oh really?' I say. He looks at me.

'Do you think if I stand you in the garden I might get a decent offer?' He's laughing.

'Not since The Big 40,' I answer.

'There you go again. Way over the top!'

He hugs me. I feel better!

Oh no!

I'm waiting for all my rosy apples to arrive. I'm looking at the board. The new board standing there with nothing to do. As bored as the last one. I'm waiting for the phone call. It's been too long now. Increased offer? No chance! I'm thinking of our other viewer. He came twice. Said all the right things. No word either. I'm used to it. Well after two years you get used to it. Well you would do if all of the three houses we've recently viewed hadn't now turned up as 'Sale Agreed.' All three of them! 'Oh no!' I say. I can hardly believe it.

'Someone's got to be making decent offers or people are still accepting lousy ones,' I tell my better-half.

'Not us!' he replies. 'I wouldn't have wanted to live in any of them, anyhow.'

'Neither would I.' I hastily agree. But there's something niggling me inside. There's something about them all being sold that makes me want them. The only difficulty I'd have now is choosing which one.

I open the front door. All my rosy apples are back from their 'tropical island.' It's lovely to see them and Pikachu of course. This huge soft cuddly yellow rotund creature with horny ears and a wavy tail leads the way.

'He sat on my table on the aeroplane,' big apple informs me.

'And did he have a lovely holiday, too?' I ask.

She pushes him at me. I hold him up. Of course I have to ask him myself.

'He says he had a super time on that tropical island,' I tell her.

'It wasn't a tropical island,' she declares. 'Tell him it was Menorca. I whisper in his ear. He feels damp. I ask why?

'He was sitting on the edge of the pool watching us swimming. We splashed him.'

'Oh no!' I say. 'He'll catch a cold.'

She is laughing. She agrees I sit him on a chair by the radiator. He'll be dry by the time she comes home from school.

I'm thinking about their 'tropical island.' I think about the sea and how compelling it is. How we are drawn to it. I think how fortunate my rosy apples are to live facing it. I think about how very nearly we came to buying a house just at its edge. Oh no! I can hardly bear the thought.

I think about our move to this house. we are just about one mile from the sea in a straight line. We almost back onto this straight line, a linear park that meets with fields and then the sea. I'm convinced we'll see it if we have a window put in the loft. We're in the middle of work anyway. We're opening the chimney for a real fire. It's not the best day for doing the work. Blowing a gale. They arrive with a chimney pot and clamber on the roof. I'm desperate to know if they'll see the sea from up there. I look at them hanging on to the chimney stack for dear life.

'Can you see the sea?' I shout up.

'Yes we'll have a cup of tea,' comes the reply.

I go in and put the kettle on. I make loft window enquiries whilst it's boiling.

Just a few years ago we spot a house on the edge of the countryside, half a mile or so, as the crow flies, from the sea. It has drawbacks but the double garage swings it for my better-half. He concedes and we move in. The biggest drawback is the lane it sides on to. It goes all the way to the shore once it's crossed the railway line. It's busy. Very busy. We plant hawthorn seedlings all the way along one hundred and twenty feet of fence. We are trying to make it private. We plant trees. The garden's looking nice. I finish it off with my planter. Reminiscent of a Grecian urn this one especially now it's old and weathered. It looks like marble as I swivel it on its plinth, careful not to cut myself on its chipped brittle plastic edges. I sink it into the gravel under the kitchen window sill. Job done.

One morning I am filled with overwhelming joy. I rush to my better-half with binoculars in hand.

'You can see the sea from the front bedroom window,' I say. He follows me upstairs. Looks across the fields to the sea wall.

'Oh so you can. Well you might see it better if the windows were cleaned. Why haven't you found a window-cleaner yet?'

I ignore it. I'm excited.

'What's covering them, anyway?' I ask.

'It's spindrift, carried by the wind from the sea.'

All of a sudden my sea-going engineer has gone poetic. Totally out of character.

'That's it!' I say. 'Right that's it. That's what we're calling it.'

'Calling what?' he asks.

'Calling the house,' I say. 'We're calling it spindrift.'

'Oh no!' he groans. 'Completely over the top! What's wrong with just having a number?'

I sense the brief poetic interlude has just come to an end.

We find a local chandler's. House names. They do house names.

We order ours in grey Cumberland stone. It will have spindrift proudly written across it in gold leaf. I can't wait for it to be ready. At last the day arrives. My better-half fixes it to the wall by the front door. I feel as though I've brought the sea to our doorstep. Not my better-half though. The refuse collectors have been. The wind's caught a few papers.

'More like bindrift,' he mumbles.

I pretend I haven't heard. I find a window-cleaner. Soon we'll be having guests. House guests for a whole week. We are entertaining an Australian business client and his wife for a whole week.

The windows are cleaned in time. Before he leaves he asks the question. I agree. He leaves his ladders in the garage.

They arrive. We arrange a gathering of like-minded people to a summer evening barbecue. I'm delighted at the opportunity to show off the new house, the garden. I forget about the lane. We are all chatting, laughing, exchanging all the niceties of life. A couple of young enthusiasts bike past. They are back again, revving for Britain. Back and forth all evening. A van stops. The driver jumps out. He's lost his way. He's shouting for directions over the fence. Suddenly lads descend in droves. Fooling around as they walk down the lane. Some drinking, hurling cans; shouting, screaming. We look up. A microlight overhead. We look up again. This time it's a powered paraglider. He's whizzing through the sky hanging from a big wing with an engine strapped to his back. There's a screech. We see the back wheel of a bicycle spinning in the air whilst the front wheel and the handlebars are firmly entrenched in the rill on the lane side of the fence. There's a helicopter circling low. The trains are hooting past. I replenish the wine glasses as fast as I can. 'Oh no!' I say. My husband is laughing. I don't think it's funny.

The next morning my better-half is off to work. Our guests are off home. I go outside. I notice the back garage door open. I look inside to see the ladders have disappeared together with many other things. I phone my better-half. He comes home to tell me he's had enough of living alongside the lane. I get ideas. Big ideas! Suddenly my sea view becomes very skimpy.

'Look,' I say. 'You know how I always wanted to live by the sea before I reached 40? Well let's do it. Now!'

'Oh no! The Roaring Forties. No thanks. Too late anyway,' he says. 'You've done The Big 40 now.'

'Too late? Never!' I retort. 'That's not fair. It was just an arbitrary deadline.'

'We'll think about it after Christmas he says.'

I am excited. The evenings have drawn in and Christmas is getting nearer. We go shopping for presents. I buy a picture. Photo-art for the new house. Just a lighthouse battling a wild sea. Oh and the lighthouse keeper standing in the doorway. It's nearly dark when we get back. My better-half looks at the kitchen window.

'Oh no!' He declares.

He strides outside with his torch. He's inspecting all the window frames. I am curious. I join him. He points the torch to the planter under the kitchen window. It's crashed to the ground. The old brittle plastic finally split in two. Compost and bulbs everywhere. He shines the light into the gravel now disturbed into one long skidding ridge. My better-half is furious.

'We could easily have walked straight into it. He's certainly had a good go at them all. Whoever it was has almost broken through this one. He could have been inside.'

'If he hadn't fallen off the planter. It went from under him, didn't it?' I say.

'Just as well,' fumes my better-half.

'Oh no! He could have hurt himself. He must have thought it was marble. Thought it would take his weight.' I suddenly see the funny side. Then it feels scary.

'We're definitely getting out of here!' My better-half means it.

It's the end of January. The house is on the market. We have much interest. I can't wait to move our spindrift sign to a more legitimate setting. We negotiate a house right on the sea-front.

'I'm not looking at that thing when we get there!'

My better-half points to the lighthouse picture. Of course I couldn't wait to hang it. I'm thinking better of it now. I know this is our once and for all, last time ever chance to be that close to the sea. Until our buyer pulls out, that is.

'Oh no!' I say.

We get another buyer. I phone the agent.

'They've withdrawn the property from the market for the time being, I'm afraid.'

'Oh no!' I say. We let our buyer go. We have no choice.

I'm browsing online. See it back on. At a higher price. Even so I'm excited. We get another buyer. Offer more money. It's accepted. We pay for the survey. We get a call from the agent.

'They've decided to sell privately to another couple, I'm afraid.'

'Oh no!' We say. We simply don't believe it!

We end up with a house one road removed and a sea view from

the back bedroom that could be slotted into the eye of a needle. We don't bother to unpack the spindrift sign. We have good reasons to move on.

Back to today. We've delivered our rosy apples to the places they go to. We walk past the boat in the front garden. I'm still thinking of the sea.

'Couldn't we just put our spindrift sign up? It would be right by the boat. At least we've got that association.' I think of the costaplenti and the dunroamin name plates. Ours would be OK.

'You've got to be joking!' Declares my better-half as the cars whiz past. 'It's the roar of the sea you want for that, not the roar of traffic. Anyhow that's going down to the sailing club. One of these days when we get round to it.'

'I want to look out of the loft window, then,' I say. 'Please.'

My better-half pulls the ladder down. With the binoculars I see a ship on the horizon. It looks like it's sailing in the sky.

'Look,' I say. I'm excited. My better-half looks.

'You'd see it a lot better if this window was cleaned,' he says.

'What's on it then?' I ask.

'Spindrift, I guess,' he replies.

I look at him and point to the grey Cumberland stone lettered in gold, half in, half out of a cardboard box alongside him.

'Someone might buy it if it's called spindrift.' I suggest.

'Oh no!' He declares. 'Don't even think of it!'

It usually happens that way!

It's half-term, but no rosy apples this week. Their daddy's mummy and daddy and the chocolate cake have travelled a long way to see them. Their daddy's mummy makes the most heavenly chocolate cake in all the world. Rosy apples can't wait for it to arrive, along with their daddy's mummy and daddy, of course.

I miss my rosy apples. We usually have a large bake-in during the school holidays. They weigh and measure and crack the eggs and mix the whole lot up with their hands before licking it off their fingers. I am reminded of my teaching days. Maths, science, language, personal and social development; there's hardly a missed area of the whole curriculum in a morning's baking. Except when they've had enough of weighing. The flour and sugar gets over-tipped. Half the drum of chocolate powder accidentally lands in one or another's bowl while I'm on my hands and knees trying to scoop up egg white and yolks escaping from shells cracked miles away from where they need to be. It usually happens that way!

Then, like magic, order from chaos. Each rosy apple in their turn popping back into the kitchen to peer through the oven glass, watching their own twelve little cakes slowly rising whilst I'm washing up.

Not this week, though. We're planning on a big family Halloween party. We'll see them then. I must think of some spooky things to do to keep them entertained.

'Any ideas?' I ask my better-half.

'You know I don't go with Halloween,' he declares.

'Better that than waiting for the phone to ring,' I answer. 'Waiting for the call from the estate agent. Thinking of a promise of a higher offer and then no word.'

'It usually happens that way!' he decides.

'Don't you think we'll hear from them again?' I ask.

'I shouldn't think so. All things considered we'll be sitting on it for a while yet.'

I agree with him. We talk about house prices. We talk about how many times we've taken advice and dropped the price to keep pace with the falling market.

'No! We've gone too low,' my better-half declares. 'We need to redress that. We need to get it back in line with the rest of them.'

I agree with him. We decide to do just that. We decide to increase the price by ten thousand pounds. We are prepared to wait for the market to stabilise. We have absolutely nothing to lose. I am filled with contentment. I decide to bake a cake.

I am thinking about baking. I am thinking about the time we were raising funds for the new community centre. We are having a summer fete. I gather my favourite relation to help me run the cake stall. I arrive late. It usually happens that way!

My cakes make me late. The last batch so over-baked they are decidedly reminiscent of little brown stones. No turning these into butterfly wings. I need to make more icing. I need to hide their brown crusting tops. My favourite relly is already there sorting out scones. I rush in and unload my masses of fairy cakes in all their variety. I am proud of them. My favourite relly pays me many compliments. I forget about the brown variegations beneath the icing as I pile them nicely alongside somebody's burnt scones. I quietly admire my handiwork as I'm thanking her. She smiles as she busies herself with paper bags and a margarine tub full of loose change.

I am getting a bit above myself. I turn to my nearest and dearest again. I am pointing at the scones.

'Look at these,' I say. 'Just look at these!'

She stops to look.

'Who would ever have dreamed of bringing these. They're burnt. They look awful!'

'I did!' she says. Her face changes. I am mortified. I am apologising and back-peddling like crazy and getting nowhere fast! I suddenly remember.

'Anyway, I should talk. You should see some of mine. The icing's hiding a multitude of sins.'

She looks at me in disbelief. 'I'll find one and show you, if you like.'

Her face breaks into a smile.

'When you get older,' she says. 'You don't care what people think.'

I return her smile. She's lovely. She makes me feel young as I approach the Big 40.

'Just you wait! What you see is what you get at my age. You'll be the same when you get older.'

Back to today. I've got my head in the fridge reaching for the eggs and butter. This is to be a very special sponge cake. One to die for. In the eyes of those who've eaten it, it's got to be able to hold its own alongside that well travelled chocolate cake. I want everyone to gasp in delight as it touches their lips.

I want to get on with it. The phone rings. It usually happens that way!

It's the estate agent.

'Can you do a viewing this afternoon?'

I hesitate. I'm baking.

'I would if I were you. They know about the increased asking price,' she advises.

I agree. My better-half groans.

'Oh no,' he says. 'I thought we were in for a prolonged period of dormancy.'

'But they know we've increased the price,' I say. 'It's unbelievable!'

'It certainly is!' He agrees. 'It usually happens that way!'

Well in reverse actually. A few years ago we were sitting on one house forever and decided it really was time to drop the price. I am about to call the estate agent. That precise moment the phone rings. Viewers! They come. They look. They are smitten. The very same day they offer us the full asking price. In the timing of a phone call we are saved from losing thousands.

Back to today. I return to my baking. I'm elated. I decide a three tier sponge is in order to mark this occasion. I must hurry up. I need to return the house to its show-home status to stand a chance.

I experience something of the joy of my rosy apples as I throw the flour from the scales to the bowl. My mind is elsewhere. An extra couple of eggs for this one. It will need more sugar. More butter. I stop weighing. I haven't the time. I'm mixing away. I'm thinking I mustn't burn this one. I remember the instant when my better-half was forced to rush home. We were socialising. Another family gathering.

'The cakes,' I panic. 'I've left a tray of cakes in the oven. I visualise the house going up in flames.

He rushes off. He rushes back to tell me off.

'Just in time,' he scolds. 'A minute later and the house would have been filled with smoke.'

I am reminded to be careful. That's not quite the way to sell a house.

I pile the mixture into the tins. There's loads left over. It usually happens that way! I find another tin. I fill it. The oven's hot and ready. They sit in pairs as they wait their turn. Soon the air will fill with that most enticing of aromas, home baking.

I rush around minimalising everywhere. It's looking like a show-house again and the cakes smell good. I wonder if I have time to make an apple pie. Then I think better of it. I think of the last time I stewed apples. Enough for an army! The necessity for more pastry grew. I'll tell you the story.

'Overdone it again?' my better-half asks.

I nod my head. It usually happens that way!

We take a slice of warm apple pie with our afternoon tea. My better-half is smiling. Now he doesn't mind.

'Very nice,' he praises. 'How many have we got?'

'Too many,' I say. 'I've baked too many. They're going in the freezer.'

He smiles at the prospect of being filled with apple pie for weeks to come.

Later on the doorbell rings. It's an old friend calling by to discuss something or other with my better-half.

'That smells good,' he says.

'Apple pie,' declares my better-half. 'She's not too bad at that.'

He tells us he's away for a few days. I promise him one on his return.

He beams. He goes. The next week he calls to collect his apple pie. I give it to him straight from the freezer. I defrost one for us. Afternoon tea and my better-half is smiling.

'And a piece of apple pie,' he says.

I check it. It's defrosted. It's gone pale and squishy. I try to cut it. I end up spooning a mushy mess onto a tea plate.

'What's happened to it?' declares my indignant better-half. 'It looks like it's taken fright!'

I think of our old friend. Then I try not to think of our old friend. I cringe in the hope I never, ever have to see him again.

Back to today. My thoughts are still negative. If it's not the apple pie, it's the trifle. I was making it for a very special occasion. A very special treat for everyone. I empty half a bottle of sweet sherry over the sponge cakes. They lap it up. It suggests the need for more! I finish it but something happens to it overnight. The glass bowl reveals thick layers of fruit-filled jelly, custard and cream. It all looks fine. I watch our first eager guest head towards it. He plunges the serving spoon deep into the whipped creamy top. Instantly he's fighting it as the jelly base swirls from under whizzing around in a pool of sweet brown sherry.

'Wow!' he says. 'That lot nearly landed on the wall.' I accept full responsibility in the hope of returning the colour to his cheeks. It did! It went down well! Like the rabbit jelly. After struggling in vain to remove it from its mould I run it under the hot water. It went down very well, never saw the light of day as it disappeared down the plug hole!

Back to today. The cakes, I take them out of the oven. All four of them less than perfect specimens. I save the least burnt one for the top. I jam them and stack them. They start to slide. They ooze masses of red strawberry jam from each circular periphery. It's looking like the leaning tower of Pisa but I've gone too far, impossible to go back now. It usually happens that way! I reach for the icing sugar. My favourite relly comes to mind. I am past the Big 40 now but I am not old enough not to care, not yet! The Big 40 hasn't changed that. I need a tin to keep it fresh. I'm on a loser. There are no cake tins in the whole of the world ever made as large as that. I think of the chocolate cake. I think I must take some lessons from my rosy apples's daddy's mummy.

'Good grief! What on earth is that? Another geological sample just like last year's Christmas cake!'

I pretend I haven't heard. 'It's for tomorrow,' I tell him.

'Trick or treat?' he asks, laughing.

'Treat!' I declare.

'As much of a treat as that apple pie. Put them together, blindfold the kids and let them poke their fingers in. You were looking for something scary to entertain them. You couldn't do better than that!'

I pretend I haven't heard. I'm looking for somewhere to hide it. We've got viewers. I don't want to frighten them off. The doorbell goes. I'm still holding it! It usually happens that way!

No most definitely not!

I am thinking fast on my feet. Very fast. I drop the shelf and bung my cake back in the oven. I answer the door to our viewers. They walk in. They admire. They absolutely love it. They leave but not before making another appointment to see it again. There and then they make a date. I am excited. This is looking so good. My better-half and I are pleased. Very pleased. It would be good to be able to put this one away. I try to capitalise on his good mood.

'Please can we have the fire lit tomorrow night? It makes such a difference to the ambience of the room, especially in the evening.'

'You've got to be joking!' he declares. 'No! Most definitely not! It's mild out there. You don't want everybody roasting. Again!'

'Again' is the operative word. Only that time summer was still lingering. We were in a different house. It had a huge inglenook fireplace. I could contain my passion to remove the old gas fire from its hearth, no longer.

'It's sacrilege,' I say. 'We must do it now. We must restore this most desirable of features to its former glory. We must do it now in time for the autumn.'

My better-half reluctantly agrees. We have the gas disconnected. We replace the baronial looking dog grate full of pretend logs with a quieter, more appropriate and most definitely empty one. This is to be filled only with the combustible products of nature!

Every day I look at it. It's summer. We are having a particularly good one. I want it to change. I want it to turn wet and cold. I want to light my fire. I want to light it now!

Suddenly it's September and a party, all at once. I pretend it's not still mild. I pretend our guests will freeze unless we light the fire.

'You'll roast us all out!' declares my better-half. 'There'll be plenty of opportunity before too long. Believe you me.'

I don't want to 'believe you me'. I want it now. I fling my arms around him and refuse to let go until he agrees.

He agrees. Our guests arrive. They love the fire. In surreptitious bursts I keep feeding it from the coal scuttle sitting in the hearth. I'm not prepared to let go of one single flame. I look around the room. People are starting to sit down. Taking jackets off, removing sweaters and woollies, stroking their foreheads, placing hands on chests, debating with top buttons. All looking flushed, turning from pink to red to crimson. My better-half returns. He's been outside talking bikes. All eyes turn to him. All eyes pleading for relief. He opens the windows, the doors. Our guests are spilling out into the night air. He removes the coal scuttle. I watch the flames go down. I watch the hot coals glow red. I watch the white ash form in dull drab swathes around the lifeless black remains.

'Never again!' declares my better-half once we've closed the front door on our last guest. 'Never again! No! Most definitely not!'

Back to today. I need to break this 'never again' barrier down. I fling my arms around him. I try negotiation.

'We'll light it later on, shall we? It is the last night in October. It is getting colder.'

He can't argue with this scientific fact. On that basis we do a deal. All our guests arrive. Rosy apples are very excited. They draw huge black spiders for me. Our utility is transformed into a

Halloween den. Our nearest and dearest present with a pumpkin. Sculptured to scary perfection. It sits in the corner flickering evil intent from its double ringed eyes, its jagged saw-edged mouth. Flickering slips of pale, meagre light into the cold dark space. I think he's done it again! This very talented relly-in-law has done it again! But that's the least of it, puremagma he is! He is the personification of creativity. I say no more except that those fortunate enough to stumble across his website are in for a treat! In the past he has been commissioned to design for the famous. His name is there for all to see. I think how lucky we girls are. Not only do our men not do the Big 40, they pool into a huge wealth of diverse talent. More on that another time.

I'm in the kitchen. A different but also very clever well-to-do relly-in-law comes in. He's asking about my new book. He's looking forward to it.

'When am I going to get to read it?' he asks. 'The first one was good. I enjoyed reading that.'

'Oh no,' I protest. 'This one definitely isn't a man's book. No! Most definitely not!'

'And why not?' he insists.

I'm struggling for words.

'The story progresses,' I say. 'It moves on. It answers all the questions. It gets very romantic. No you wouldn't enjoy it at all.'

I go hot all over. I want to die. I want to disown it. I wish I'd toned it down now.

He looks at me. 'Tell me,' he says. 'Are there any of your own experiences in it?'

'No! Most definitely not!' I hastily reply. 'It's based purely on imagination.'

He looks like he doesn't believe me. He won't let go.

'I had a friend who wrote a book once. I actually proof read it for him. Good story. He told me it was part made up. Part based on his own experiences. I find it most strange that you say there is nothing of you in your book. It's alright you know. You can tell me.'

'Well there isn't!' I repeat. 'No! Most definitely not!' I insist.

This charismatic man walks away. Another joker in the pack! I know he doesn't believe me. I am struggling to handle this kitchen-based fame. I fear for it spreading to the lounge.

The doorbell rings. We don't do Halloween. I'm still floundering as my better-half tells me to answer it.

'No! Most definitely not!' I declare. I refuse to be bossed about by an insistent man.

He rushes past me to the utility. He rushes back shaking the coffin shaped box of sweet body pieces. In the coffin window, eyes, noses and teeth all wrapped in luminous green cellophane. I get on with heating the food. I need the oven. I brave the evil orange face as it lights up my four storey cake. I take it outside and leave it there. I don't want to attract any more attention.

The doorbell goes again. The cardboard coffin makes its way down the hall. I'm pleased. I'm dodging it all quite nicely. I persuade my better-half to light the fire. All eyes turn to the blaze. The doorbell rings again. I look at my better-half.

'No! Most definitely not!' he states. 'It's your turn now!'

'No! I'm not going!' I insist.

'Open it!' He demands. He means it. I rush to the door, then stop. I dash past him to grab the coffin box of body pieces gleaming in the light thrown from the orange evil face. Big apple wants to see who's there. I come rushing into the hall. She opens the door. From the darkness I see a hand holding a big bunch of flowers. I see a face. He's smiling. I am momentarily stunned. I am looking at my intelligent, witty, famous politician. He of all I would most like to meet in the whole world! Our guests have gathered into an audience behind me. They are laughing. I kiss this life-size cardboard cut-out and graciously accept his gift. I am holding the flowers. I step back in amazement. Suddenly from this handsome congenial face I see two long fangs appear. The teeth of Dracula. I jump! My very talented relly-in-law is pulling the strings. I all but collapse in a heap. We are overcome with shrieks of laughter. We are rolling around.

'I'll use it for my book launch,' I laugh. 'They say the only way is to get a celebrity!'

'Or be photographed with one!' Somebody says as the camera clicks.

'No! Most definitely not!' I declare. Too late! We are photographed together. Nobody hears. There is too much laughter.

Sunday morning. We agree. Halloween turned out to be a good night. Just the ashes in the hearth now. It's cold, wet and windy out there.

'Can we have the fire again tonight?' I ask my better-half. He looks at my famous politician lying by the hearth.

'Only if you're up for doing a Harriet on the rug,' he laughs.

'No! Most definitely not!' I reply. I wonder just what it is with the men in our family at the moment.

No question about it!

We close the door on our viewers. This is the third time they've been. They want it. They actually want to buy it but they have a house to sell in London. That's OK. That's fine. We are in no hurry. Christmas is looming and there is shopping to be done. But who's to say they won't get a buyer today, tomorrow?

'Don't build your hopes up too much,' says my better-half. 'It's not in the bag yet.'

'But who's to say?' I reply. 'They loved it. There's no question about it!'

I am excited. I read in the Sunday paper there's a shortage of properties for sale. I'm wondering if this serious shortage starts in London. We need to look around again. Just in case. We make appointments to view three more. We come home. We rate them out of ten. Eight, seven and five. We have two serious contenders, assuming of course they're still available at the critical time. I don't want to see any more 'Sale Agreed' signs ahead of us.

I am thinking about Harriet. I am thinking about relationships and the twists and turns they can take. I am thinking about how very sad it is when houses have to be sold because the twists and turns spiral to leave one reluctant partner not wanting to go. One reluctant partner left with half the proceeds. Left with half a life and half the money to try to make it work. It is a beautiful house we've viewed, but as with my lost diamond, there's an ethical issue looming with number seven.

I mustn't steep in empathy. I must get on with planning my

shopping. I'm Christmas shopping early this year to leave time to organise a party. A party to celebrate the launch of my new book.

I am thinking of this as we are walking hand in hand along the seafront. The sky is as bright and as clear as if it were a summer's day. The tide's just gone out leaving a mass of small pools in the dips of wet sand. The seagulls gather for morning assembly then lift off, swooping low to land, sinking webbed feet into the shallow cold water left behind by the sea. It reminds me of Christmas. It reminds me of Christmas Day, nearly always sunny. I am thinking of Harriet. I am thinking of Harriet and Mark's Christmas. Of course it's not an ordinary Christmas Day for them. When does Harriet ever do ordinary? So, for my readers, I want it to be an extra surprise to delight them. I want 'Ne Obliviscaris' to be at the top of their Christmas list.

Back to shopping. I am thinking of one particular time not too long ago. I think of the hassle. I think of leaving the house almost before the first bird awake has had time to trill from somewhere in the tree-lined road. I think of the car parks in town, already full to overflowing. I think of my better-half frowning as he squeezes the car into a less than desirable parking slot.

'Right,' he declares as he's sticking the ticket on the inside of the windscreen. 'We've got three hours. If you haven't done it by them you're not going to.'

The pavements are crowded. The shops are crowded. The check-outs are crowded. I haven't a clue what anyone wants.

'We need some trays,' I declare. On this particular Christmas we are having guests to stay.

'I want it to be like a hotel,' I say. 'I want to be able to offer tea-making facilities. It will make their stay far more enjoyable. There's no question about it!'

'Tea-making facilities!' declares my better-half. 'I don't believe it! How easy is it for everyone to get to the kitchen?'

'It doesn't matter,' I insist. 'We've already got the kettles. Just a little milk, teabags, sugar. That's all it takes. Now I need some new trays. In here. We'll get them in here.'

We go into the unsuspecting shop. My better-half knows there is no stopping me. We wend our way through the crowds and finally I spot them. Absolutely perfect. Tons of them all differing designs resting upright on a very long, almost out-of-reach shelf. Just one or two people down this end.

'Oh look,' I say. Amongst the wide variety of designs I spot perfection. There's no question about it! Masses of little holly-leaves totally covering these rectangular masterpieces.

'We really don't need any more trays, especially tin ones.'

I can hear my better-half being overcome with Christmas shopping grump. I pretend not to hear. I will not let him spoil this moment of delight.

'Right,' I say, pointing at the ones covered in holly leaves and bright red berries. 'Two of those. I'm having two of those.'

'If you must,' he retorts. He's moving away. I see him bending a little. He's got his head down pretending to scan the lower shelves below the counter housing a multitude of kitchen electricals. I know he's trying not to be part of this 'must have' thing.

'Yes, I must,' I reply. I am talking to myself whilst stretching on tip-toes to reach them. I feel the raised rim in my hand. I try to pull them towards me. Then nightmare city! Like one of those world-beating domino events they set one another off. They clang and bang in loud, ear piercing metal clusters to the floor. Discordant, deafening, setting nerves on edge noise fills the whole shop. Worse than those never-ending banging fireworks. A continuous clanking and clattering until the last one goes. Mercifully they miss all the electricals displayed on the counter. I see the whole of the shop gather round. People rushing to the scene. People pointing, staring, going 'Ooooh! Arrrh! Just look at those!'

I daren't look round to my better-half. I'm on my hands and knees picking them up. I meet him half way round. He's passing them to an assistant. The crowd gradually disperses. I am apologising profusely. I am saying how difficult they were to reach. My better-half is nudging me, pointing to the rows of shelves below. I wonder what's the matter with him.

'Which ones were you wanting?' I get asked. There was no sense of the joy of Christmas in her tone.

'Oh those please,' I say. 'Two of the same please.'

She passes me two from the gathered-up pile without a smile.

'I'll take these to the check-out then,' I say. She nods. I'm more than anxious to get away from this disastrous scene.

'I couldn't help it,' I say, trying to pre-empt my better-half's reaction. 'Anyway it might have been better if you'd tried to get them for me. Disappearing just when I needed help!'

'Disappearing!' He objects.

'Yes! Disappearing! There's no question about it!'

'Disappearing indeed! I was trying to find what you wanted. Didn't you see them stacked on the shelves under the counter?'

'No!'

I go quiet. I feel bad. We pay for them.

'Let's go to the book shop now,' I suggest. He looks at me.

'As long as you don't touch anything,' he declares.

I pretend I haven't heard.

Back to today. I'm not taking any chances. Online shopping for me now. There's no question about it! You can't go wrong with that. Well I say you can't go wrong, but you can. Oh yes you can! I remember spotting a 'Brand New With Tags' sheepskin jacket. It was to be the perfect Christmas present for my better-half. I bid. I want it. I bid up. In my desire to win it I increase my bid. I am told to enter my maximum amount. I do. I'm in a hurry. Time is running out. It's bidding up. I put the decimal point in the wrong place. Suddenly I am offering five hundred pounds and thirty pence for this ideal gift. I nearly die. I panic. I must bear this misfortune alone. The auction has three minutes to run. I am hoping no one out there is as desperate for this jacket as me. I am hoping no one out there will be one bid away from the life-changing sum I've just staked. I can hardly bear to watch as the seconds tick by. I win it. I win it at a price that renders my decimal point insignificant. The relief! I can't believe it. Had it been my lost diamond my bid could easily have been swallowed up. I could easily have been the winner! I could well have been one of those suffering the misfortune of a downward spiralling relationship. I could well have been digging one of those kind of holes for myself that Harriet is so good at!

The phone rings. It's the estate agent wanting to know what we thought of property number eight.

'We like it very much,' I say. 'We'd certainly like a second viewing if it's still available when we get an offer.'

My better-half appears.

'We've just had the agent on the phone wanting to know what we thought about the house we viewed.'

'Which one?' he asks. 'We saw three.'

'Oh you know,' I tell him. 'The one with the two ensuites and the bathroom. A bathroom for each bedroom. Come to think of it we'd only need tea-making facilities, then it would be just like a hotel for the next time we do Christmas.'

'Oh no,' groans my better-half. 'Not those dented trays again!'

'Dented?' I query. 'Who did that, then?'

'You did, remember? Hadn't you noticed?'

I pretend not to hear. I'm not up for handling the implications of his unfortunate observation. I can't bring myself to go there.

Back to the task in hand. I'm browsing. I'm thinking about the family. Gifts to meet hobbies, gifts of fashion, books and music. Gifts for him, gifts for her. Gifts for the young. Gifts for the elderly and everyone else in between. I spot some stereotyping going on here. Oh no! Not that Big 40 again! It has no part to play in Christmas shopping. No! I simply refuse. I will not give my one-generation-removed relly-in-law a pair of comfy bobbled slippers. She shall have Harriet to enjoy over Christmas. She'll soon discover that Harriet doesn't do The Big 40 either. She'll soon discover that these days nobody needs to. There's no question about it!

Golly gosh!

This morning rosy apples are late. Their mummy arrives in a spin.

'Calamity!' she declares.

I wonder what could be amiss until I discover little apple's been throwing a tantrum. In a strop because she can't put on her mermaid doll's plastic double-D, or thereabouts. The poor thing might be used to waving her fishtail against the watery rocks but without that she'll surely freeze! So rosy apple's mummy has been struggling away with this preformed perverse strip of plastic, to oblige.

'Golly gosh!' I'm thinking. 'When I used to play with dolls they had nappies and bottles. These days they make them well on their way to The Big 40.'

We've got a birthday party tonight. It's very creative relly-in-law's birthday. Rosy apples tell me they are looking forward to it. Well they would. Very creative relly-in-law has always got something up his sleeve to keep them amused. Keep us all amused. I'm looking at my famous politician propped up against the office wall. I've managed to swing those fangs well out of sight. I'm thinking that's a joke too far!

I'm steeped in thought as we take rosy apples to where they all go. I'm thinking how fortunate are those authors who can actually secure a celebrity for their book launch. Still, I'm more than realistic. I'll go with my cardboard one just as long as I can keep those fangs well out of the way!

We are on our way home now. We are almost at the drive.

Suddenly I spot that house down the road. The one that got sold. The board's back again.

'Golly gosh!,' I utter to my better-half. 'I wonder what that's all about?'

I can just see the scenario. I'm thinking about our potential buyers. I'm thinking..... Well, no, I don't even want to go there. But I need reassurance.

'It would happen that way. I don't believe it!' I continue. My better-half's reading my mind.

'It's unpredictable,' he declares. I can tell by his expression he's not about to enter into lengthy debate. I go online. I check it out. It's still reading 'Sale Agreed'. I am suffering from online confusion.

I think on it no more. I must get on with Christmas shopping. I'm back online. I've asked for a list. I have it in front of me. All my rosy apples' heartfelt desires. Pokemon leads the way. Big apple is desperate for one of those square boxes that sit on shop counters, stacked to bursting with sealed packs of those world famous must-have cards. I'm heading for my favourite auction. There might be a deal to be done. I spot them. 'Buy it Now' or 'Best Offer'. Golly gosh! I decide I will make a 'Best Offer'. At that price this guy's wisdom is undoubtedly revealed. I umm and aah. It's too much money. There's no photograph. I change my mind. I google it. Almost double the price! Wow! This guy's giving them away! I return to his website. Make a best offer. Now I am waiting.

I go back to the rest of the list. I'll call her Princess Glam. She's next and then it's her buddy Princess Ourus. Golly gosh! Two more of them both looking as though their Double-D's are nowhere near adequate! I wonder what's happened to childhood. Littlest apple is only three! I'm relieved to get back to Lucario of Pokemon. No letters of the alphabet for this one. I look at his face. Golly gosh! He's enough to scare all these plastic girls back into their Christmas wrapping paper.

I'm checking my in-box. Mail! My offer's rejected. He comes back with a counter-offer. I decline. He invites me to try again. I accept his invitation to up it and return to those dolls.

Brilliant! With hardly a scroll I find an online store stocking the lot. I go for it. I get to the check-out. I part with my details. Then I don't believe it! Golly gosh! Such a personal question pops up. I struggle with it. I ignore the box. I carry on and click the 'Proceed to next stage' button. It comes hurtling back. A command in red letters. 'This is a required field'. I ignore it and try again. No, it's back! I can see I'm not going to get anywhere with this one. I empty my virtual shopping basket. I'll go elsewhere. I'll find an online store that is polite and blessed with good manners.

I check my emails again.

'Ah! This has to be better news this time,' I'm thinking. No! Not a bit of it. I'm reading 'Offer rejected! Try again.' I leave it for the moment.

I'm getting nowhere fast. I return to that store. I email them and tell them I wish to override this most intrusive of questions. I'm pinged an immediate response. Absolutely no response! In my opinion. I decide on a final email. 'No thank you,' I write, 'I shall seek to purchase these items else where.' I seek but I do not find. I'm clicking on every Double-D doll that ever graced the internet and I'm still getting nowhere fast. I go searching for my better-half. I explain my dilemma. He's laughing.

'Oh put it in my name,' he says. 'I don't know what your problem is!'

Well he wouldn't would he? I've already told you the men in our family don't do The Big 40!

I am so thankful this is an online store. So much better than face to face! No, when things go wrong, face to face isn't the place to be. I'll tell you about it. I'm popping into a small local shop, now well closed and turned into something else. He sells the most delicious boiled ham. I go in. He's beaming. I'm a regular customer, We always chat, set the world to rights, that kind of thing. But this particular morning I go in. The shop's empty. He stops the conversation whilst I pay for my ham. Then he's looking at me.

'Not bad for an oldie,' he's suddenly saying.

Golly gosh! I don't know whether to be pleased or annoyed. 'I'm not quite at the Big 40, yet,' I'm thinking. I want to change the subject. I find myself telling him how special his boiled ham is. I find myself telling him it's the best boiled ham for miles around. I'm asking him where it comes from? What makes it so different?

'I do it myself,' he replies. 'I've got one on the go now. I'll show you.' Instantly I am marched round the back. I peer into this large bubbling pot. I don't want to be there. I don't want to know his scientific method for boiling it. His stove is right by the door. He's blocking the doorway. I want to get out. I want to get out now! We hear the shop door open, then again and again. I am so relieved. He wants to get back to his customers. He wipes both hand down the side of his sparkling white apron. I see faces. I see smiling faces.

'I've been showing her how I boil my ham.' He's laughing.

I grab my ham off the counter and rush out. 'I won't be going in there for a while,' I'm thinking.

Back to today. I'm looking at my latest email.

'No more chances to offer on this item. Don't let it get away! Buy it now before someone else does.'

I panic. I press the button. I've bought it. I check my list. It says Pokemon EX. I check the web page. It just says Pokemon. Where's the EX? I scan the page. It's not written anywhere. Golly gosh! I've just spent a fortune and I've bought the wrong one! I'm still panicking. I can't do anything about it now. I hope against hope there'll be an EX somewhere on the box. When it arrives. I'll just have to wait. To see. What with these things and Double-D dolls. It's just not fair on the likes of us who've past the Big 40! I daren't tell my better-half. This is definitely not one of my better days for online shopping.

He's online shopping, too. I hope he's having better luck. His is car insurance. How boring is that! Well at least you can't go wrong with it. Or can you? Suddenly I hear him not being very polite.

'Bl- - dy wonderful,' I hear him say as he's mounting the stairs. He arrives, laughing.

'I thought I was talking to one of those recorded messages again!'

'Don't swear,' I say. 'It's not very nice. I do hope you apologised.'

'You shouldn't have to, to get a decent service,' he replies. I keep very quiet. My errors are all of my own making!

I go back to that store. I place the order on behalf of my better-half and hope the recipient of my final email isn't looking. Within minutes, three in a row. Three emails all from that store. I'll get round to opening them, but not today! I've had enough for today. We've got a party to go to!

My dearest relly has had much better luck with her online shopping than me. Her buffet is divine, heavenly! In truth, we all agree, 'This is not just food, this is truly More? & Seconds? food. This is the epitome of temptation. We wine, dine and laugh the evening away. I'm asked about my new book. The party to launch it and when it's likely to be. Suddenly I get cold feet. Those characters! They've taken on a life of their own! I can't have invited guests thinking I've gone wayward. No! We'll just make it an ordinary party. Just an ordinary Christmas party. I'll leave the publicity to all places online.

It's time to go home.

'Oh, I've got something for you,' says my very creative relly-in-law.

He gives me a small photograph. Golly gosh! I'm standing up and close alongside this 'famous person whom I would most like to meet' with my bunch of flowers. He has closed in. His head is leaning towards mine. We are an item! My creative relly-in-law has worked on this halloween image to perfection. Well, not quite! I am delighted until I spot those fangs! Delighted until he gives me a set of white fanged teeth.

'Body bits!' he says

'Oh no,' I think, 'plastic body bits! Not more!'

I can't believe I've wasted most of the day looking for plastic bodies wearing plastic Double-D bits. I'm suffering from online confusion. I'm suffering from online intrusion. I'm suffering from

The Big 40! Oh and now my feet are freezing!

No! I just can't go with that!

It's a new day! A new start! I'm filled with optimism. The board down the road is showing off a 'Sale Agreed' sign and I've been so well praised on my favourite auction. Invited back to 'Shop here for Pokemon, anytime!' And I've actually managed to create a party invitation from all that stuff that's already sitting in the computer when you first buy it. Oh it started! Yes it started again though. It just came up with one in the corner of the page when I printed it off and I wanted four. Now I'm playing about. Low and behold I get four! I'm flying! Next, what to call it? Christmas Party? Open House? Book Launch? No! I just can't go with that! What if nobody turns up? I don't want to put them off before they've hardly had chance to open the envelopes. I'm struggling. I must put this fear of publicity behind me. I have a better idea! Our Christmas party will double up. Double up as a book launch. I won't tell them though. I'll see how it goes. Hide a couple of books and then if someone else mentions it I'll bring them out. I must consult my all-things-wise better-half on this one, though. This is too important to get wrong. But not now. Not today. The car's due for its MOT. He's got other things on his mind. He's thinking how long can he stall its replacement.

Back to Christmas shopping. I'm still at it! You wouldn't believe how I could still be at it! I'm looking at my rosy apples' Christmas list. No! I've got it wrong! I've missed the car. Princess Glam must come with a car. The trouble with this one is she changes her models at the slightest whim. I steel myself for a return visit to that online store. No! I haven't opened my emails yet! I am thinking it's probably better if I don't! At the moment I can only find one and that's sitting in its box with this determined Princess standing alongside it. Ready for the off! No! Wrong colour! I'm not going there again. I'm still waiting for that 'sits on the top of the counter' box of Pokemon cards to arrive. Still waiting to see if I'll be able to find that unmentioned 'EX'. I can't afford to fudge it again.

I'm taking refuge in my favourite auction. I'm scrolling away. All types and makes of these things are appearing. Not new though, unless of course I go for 'A nearly new never been played with' one. No! I just can't go with that! It must be new. It must be brand new. I'm scrolling down. I'm getting nowhere. I come out. I start googling. I see one. I see the price. I'm moving on. I'm moving on in disbelief! It looks like it's going to have to be that nearly new one after all. I go back. It's got one of these dolls sitting in it. All raring to go! All raring to drive off to somewhere more exciting than is good for her. No! I can't be doing with another of these Double-D dolls. In any case I can't give one without the other. If Princess Glam's going to have a mate, then so it must be for Princess Orous. I come out. I move on. Page after page. I'm now glancing the margins to the right of the screen. I'm promised my exact requirements. I can't find one. I decide this much desired car has been rendered obsolete. That explains it! That explains the price!

I go back to my auction. I must waste no more time. I buy it! I've settled for an extra one of these materialistic Double-D dolls in order to get the first one a new car. They'll have to toss up as to which one's to sit behind the steering wheel. She may have no choice. I'm bringing the picture up of the one I've already bought. Oh no! It looks like the wrong doll! It looks like her legs don't bend. She's standing tall next to her large freezer. Totally disinterested! 'A takeaway tonight,' comes to mind. Just like Harriet! It looks like her new buddy won't even need to budge over. It looks like she'll be doing the driving if they're ever going to get anything to eat.

I'm thinking it might be better for driving if they'd been wearing jeans and a comfy navy-blue jumper. Like the one I used to wear. Only when home of course, doing the housework. On my own at home. I'll tell you about it.

It's a grocery store again. Much further afield this one. Now no longer, of course.

'The other one?' You might ask.

Well you wouldn't have expected me to go back into that one, would you? Not so soon, anyway. I still haven't reached The Big 40 but it's starting to get to me. I'm baking. I run out of flour. Oh and I need some ham. I'm in my jeans and a one size too big navy jumper. This guy's looking particularly miserable today. He's had better days. Oh, I've popped in there on the way home from work on the odd occasion. I've popped in there for something or other I've forgotten to get. I've popped in with my high-heeled shoes on and a pretty blouse under a work suit, just on the very rare occasion. He's always smiled. Pleasantly passed the time of day. But not today. No definitely not today. He looks like he's got something on his mind, today. I go in.

'Are you alright there lad?' I hear him saying.

'But I'm not a lad!' I'm protesting to myself. I'm breathing in.

Standing straight. Desperately trying to utilise my feminine assets. A bit like those dolls I've just been shopping for. Only nothing so glamorous!

I'm standing there, frozen in disbelief. 'No! It's definitely not right! To call me that. My hair's long as well. If there's one thing I'm not it's a lad. I don't look like one! I don't act like one! My better-half, he's the man in our house. He does all things manly. I believe in it. Men things for men! Girl things for girls! No! My better-half can vouch for it. And I'm most definitely a girl! Surely this guy's contact lenses have misted up, or something? He's seen me before. How can he possibly suddenly think I'm a lad?'

This time I know whether to be pleased or annoyed. I'd leave but he's already heaved his ham shank onto the slicing machine. Boy is he taking his time! His eyes are distant. He's looking over the top of my head.

'You know what it's like, don't you?' He's saying. 'They just can't stop spending. She wants this and that all the time. She never stops. Oh I don't know what I'm going to do about it. Let me tell you what she's after now…'

I'm looking nervously out of the window towards my car parked right outside. He gets the message. This is not going to be one of those guys to lads chats. He's speeded up his slicing. I pay and look behind. I see a lad sauntering out of the adjacent aisle. He continues telling him his woes as I'm leaving the shop. I'm overwhelmed with relief! I go home. I've forgotten the flour. I don't mind. It's totally insignificant. I must do one thing. I must do it now! I must get changed.

I'm looking like Princess Glam. I've abandoned baking. I'm

hoovering away looking like Princess Glam. I'm faltering my way towards The Big 40. I decide it's the wrong time of life to dive out looking like that. I should have known. He was looking over the top of my head. He was looking at the rashers of ham slowly falling into the greaseproof paper sitting in the flat of his hand but he wasn't looking at me. I'm feeling better and I'm not. All at once! I go back to the hoovering. I can't settle. I switch it off. I need some flour. I need some reassurance. I'm on my way to my local shop. The other one. The one I'd decided to leave well alone. I'll just make sure I stay this side of the counter!

Back to today. I can still feel the relief. Definitely not one of my better off-days, that one. The sort of day that starts so full of promise then goes rapidly down hill. The sort of day I'm having at the moment thanks to these glamorous girls.

I must turn to Princess Orous. Little apple is surely going to need a car for her. I'm back on google. I'm back on my favourite auction. I'll find one with a chum already behind the wheel. Just like middle apple's. Slight problem! There's no car to be had. No car with a chum anywhere. Unlike her buddy. Or is it her buddy's buddy? I'm confused! She can't get enough of them. She tosses them away like sweetie papers. I bring up the picture. This Princess Orous doesn't look like she's prepared to bend her knees, let alone drive. She's standing like a poker alongside her bath. Can't wait to get in it. Can't wait to while away her time lazing and soaking.

I'm back on google. I'm checking to see if her legs will bend. I'm spending ages on it. I'm getting nowhere fast. I give up! I look for accessories instead. Any accessories for this low difficult doll.

Ah! At last! A pack of outfits. I 'Buy it Now!' Little apple likes dressing dolls. I'm making progress. I'm making progress until I'm pinged an email. 'Please don't pay for this item. None in stock.' This is a request to agree cancellation. I'm back to square one. No, it's even worse. I've got to go back in and sort that one out. So this doll's not even going to get a clean change of clothes. There's absolutely nothing I can buy for this awkward Princess. No! If that's the way she wants it she can sit all day and all night in her bath. In her ball gown in her bath. On her own! As she's no change of clothes. She can sit until her dress is laundered! She needs some life experience this doll. If ever there was a case for jumper, jeans and a working hoover, this is it! Anyway, far more fun for the kids!

Rosy apples' mummy has just arrived. She wants to know what I've bought for her apples so we don't double-up. We get to the non-listed impromptu things. 'Oh no!' She says. 'Oh I've just auctioned some of those. She's grown out of those now.' She moves on. 'Oh and that. She's already got one exactly the same. She's never bothered with it much. I've just auctioned that one too.'

Oh no! I've now got to re-jig my Christmas shopping. I've wrapped them. I've labelled them. They're all sitting in a box in the loft. I seek my better-half. He'll need to get them down. He's been under the car. He's washing his hands in the utility. It looks like he's finished with all that now. Dare I mention our Christmas double-up as well? I've got invitations to be getting on with. He greets me.

'It's no good,' he says. 'If we're lucky we might get another year out of it. I doubt it though.'

I smile. 'Oh, I've found us one,' I say.

'Oh yes?' He looks at me suspiciously. 'You're not still after getting Sanderson's silver Mercedes, are you?'

I laugh. 'Well it would be nice, very nice. His is top of the range though. I couldn't pretend to be Harriet sitting in anything less!'

'In your dreams!' he replies.

'You don't like him do you?' I cautiously suggest.

'No! He's a chauvinist! A bourgeois spiv!'

No! I just can't go with that! I will not have Mr Sanderson maligned. 'He just needs a little understanding, that's all,' I say.

'You what? Understanding! I don't believe I'm hearing this!'

I can see he's laughing but I'm of a mind to stay quiet. I decide this is not the best time for asking him about my book launch. I go back to safer ground. I go back to talking cars.

'No, not a silver Mercedes. I was joking. I found a different one. For a doll!. Absolutely silly price!'

He laughs, puts his arm round me. 'That's OK we'll go for one of those then, if you want to role play. You'll need to glam up a bit though. You won't have to be sitting by me in those jeans and that jumper.'

'Hardly!' I reply. This is one joke I don't want to get. 'Seeing as neither of us would fit in!'

'Of course we would,' he replies. 'Haven't you seen any of those going past yet?'

He's still laughing. I look at my jeans and jumper. Bad memories! I'm going to get changed. No! I just can't go with that!

Too clever by half!

I wake up. I make a decision. Today I will glam up. Nothing over the top of course. Just a more attractive jumper. Plain, dark blue, fitted with a deep V-neck so I can wear a pretty top underneath. Don't get me wrong! It's got nothing to do with those cars. No, I'm just not up for sitting alongside my better-half in one of those. No! If I glam up a bit. Just a bit and suggest we do the garages, I might conceivably find a silver Mercedes to get up and close to. But it's got to be a silver Mercedes. Exactly like Mr. Sanderson's. I know just what I want. I've read the brochure inside out This is some fantastic car! Like his boat really, but we'll leave buying one of those for another time!

Now, I've got to tell you how disappointed I am though. So disappointed our car passed its MOT. Wouldn't you know! It could have obliged and failed. We could have ditched it. Bought another! I'd have saved my better-half the bother of looking around. No! I'd have found him one straight away. I've been on the look out for ages. Ever since Harriet first stepped into his. Still! There's a glimmer of hope on the horizon! But for now I must stop dreaming. I must get on with the day.

I find my jumper, inside out. I'd put it away inside out. I'm in a hurry. I struggle to pull the sleeves through to the right side. Oh no! It's covered in white bits! White bits, would you believe! A snow storm of them. White bits everywhere! I'm shaking it. I'm shaking this now spotty newly collaged jumper furiously.

'What on earth are you doing?' I'm met with my better-half.

'Don't ask!' I declare.

'Not again! Why don't you check it instead of just throwing it all in? You'll never learn! No logic!'

I don't want to learn. I don't want to be logical. My better-half is blessed with too much logic. He's too clever by half! Who wants to spend time rummaging in pockets and up sleeves for tissues? Not me! I'd rather be writing! I'm putting it on. I'm brushing the bits off as I go. I must get on with the day.

I'm looking out of the window. It's that big black cloud again. It's pouring down! We're waiting for the delivery van. The weekly shop. It arrives. The poor man rings the doorbell. He's soaked but cheerful. 'Magic,' he says as I'm thanking him. My better-half doesn't think so. He's looking at the line of heaving carrier bags sitting the length of the hall. Soaking wet carrier bags.

'All yours,' he says. Then he disappears.

I'm shoving all this stuff into the freezer. Into the fridge. Into the cupboards. I'm in a hurry. I don't want to be here. Here in the kitchen. In the kitchen doing this. I want to be on my computer. I've got shopping to finish. I'm crashing along. Down to the last item. The last item in the last carrier bag. Flour! Memories! I'm momentarily distracted. I'm balancing this large unwieldy bag high on one hand whilst trying to rummage space in the wall-cupboard with the other. I can feel it going. Oh no, I can feel it going! Bang onto the worktop. Bang onto the floor! Split bag. Flour everywhere! I'm covered! I look like I've escaped from one of those filled with water magic Christmas glass snow shakers. I close the kitchen door. I must hide all this from my better-half. I hear the back door open. He's in!

'What on earth are you doing now?' he says.

I'm trying to explain. 'That's the carrier bag. It was the last thing in that. I was just trying to put it away.'

He's looking inside. He's running his hand along the inside of the bottom. It's covered in flour.

'The bag was already split,' he declares. Didn't you notice?'

'No! We're not all as observant as you! Too clever by half!' I say.

He's laughing as he walks away. I clear it up. I'm in a bad mood! My attempts to glam up have been finally sabotaged by a bag of flour. I decide there's absolutely nothing 'magic' about today!

I'm getting changed. I'm changing into last night's evening jumper because it's there. And we might just get to go out. Get to do those garages!

Last night we were round at rosy apples' house. Rosy apples' house with a fire half-way up the chimney. It was something else. Roaring away on driftwood from the beach. No chocolate brown Labrador jumping at the window tonight. I feel bad! This dog can't join the party. Because of me. This dog's in the kitchen because of me. This gorgeous dog is not a problem. When it's not near me, of course. It's exuberance is more than scary. Much more than scary! I haven't yet got the hang of this dog's way of greeting humans!

It was little apple's fourth birthday. She was having a party to celebrate. Wining and dining again! It's caught on. Rosy apples' mummy was also serving not just food. We were all up for More & Seconds! Didn't need asking twice! We're sitting there. All of a sudden middle apple is stretching up. Reaching across me for two long dangling legs scaling the book shelves. This one's trying to catch up with her buddy. She pulls them both down. Oh no! More of those Double-D dolls! I suggest she gets them dressed for fear of them catching cold. She's not listening. She's doing a Christmas present reckie.

'I hope you've got my doll and the car and a long dress for her?' she's saying. 'If ever two dolls need long dresses, it's these two,' I'm thinking. She dumps these naked, rigid creatures on my lap. 'It's a priority!' I decide to myself. 'It's vests and knickers for these girls tomorrow!'

We are chatting, laughing, enjoying the evening. We are looking out at the black night sky. We see headlights on the sand. Rosy apples' daddy tells us they're bringing the lifeboat in. It's exciting! Romantic! It reminds me of Harriet. I'm thinking how much I want my readers to let Harriet take them into her dreams. Take them through the answers to all the questions. Take them every step of the emotional way right to the very end. From the comfort of their sofa over Christmas I want them to discover if it ever works out for Harriet. I want them to read 'Ne Obliviscaris'.

Time quickly steals away this pleasant evening. We are leaving. They are all patting the dog. The dog on the other side of the kitchen gate. On the other side of the gate because of me. I need to join in. I need to brave this lively dog. Its head is back. Its eyes are crossing backwards towards its ears. I hover. I go for it. I see yards of pink tongue lolloping from its mouth. I freeze. It licks me. We are friends! I savour this new experience as we cross the road to the car. As I watch my better-half trying to open the boot. He's turning the key. It's swivelling round. He's delving under the dashboard. The car's shaking and clattering. He's coming back.

'The dog licked me!' I'm telling him.

'Huh!' he says. 'Electronics!'

I pretend to sympathise. I'm secretly delighted! I'm asking myself how can we cope with a hammering, noisy boot-lid? A boot-lid in perpetual motion. A boot-lid that will only open from somewhere obscure. From somewhere obscure under the dashboard.

'We definitely need a new car.' I suggest. 'We need a silver Mercedes.'

'Oh no we don't!' My better-half retorts. 'We've more than likely got a house move to contend with!'

I pretend I haven't heard. I'm thinking the more things that go wrong with this, the better!

Back to today. I'm online hiding from my better-half. I'm scrolling down. I'm trying to find underwear for these offending dolls. They must sell it somewhere! I'm deviating. I've got other things to do. I can feel the day falling apart. I've got my better-half's Christmas present list in front of me. I go to the website. I decide it's got to be the most boring website in the world. I'm reading the list. I'm looking at the pictures. I can't tell one from the other. I'm struggling. Struggling hard to get it right. I suggested a telescope, a new camera, a notebook, a laptop even. But no! What am I battling to find? Motorbike bits! That's what he wants. He's given me a list the length of the road. My mind is elsewhere. My mind is still searching for doll's clothes. I envisage having to get that spooky sewing machine out. I'll be sewing away on Christmas Eve. No! I'm just not prepared to give more of these lacking in essential garments Doule-D dolls out as presents on Christmas Day unless they're respectable through and through!

I'm deviating. I'm back to the list. I keep putting things like wires and screws and nuts and bolts and gaskets and sumps and washers into the basket. This is the dullest virtual basket I'm ever having the misfortune to fill. Now if I were looking for diamonds that would be different!

I'm finished! At last I'm finished. I go to the checkout. I part with my details. No personal questions from this guy! This guy's online store might be dull but at least he's blessed with good manners. I proceed with confidence. It's closure! I'm reading a 'Thank you for your custom, you will receive a confirmation email shortly,' notice.

The phone rings. It's our other set of nearest and dearest rellies. These two are also clever and talented but it doesn't end there. Not with these two. They are also the bravest of the brave! I can't compete! My dearest relly-in-law is incredibly brave in her own right. But the problem is her better-half. He's my elder-sibling-relly. He bagged all the brave genes first. Oh he managed to save a few for my middle-sibling-relly. She got some, but I didn't get any. They'd all been bagged by the time I came along. Not one left for me! Not even one! I don't do brave. Brave isn't part of my life! As you've already discovered.

My better-half arrives. I relate the call.

'We've been invited over for lunch before Christmas.'

'Oh jolly good!' he says.

I'm looking at him. his hands are full of boring bits.

'But they live in a nice house. In a nice part. We can't go driving through one of the smartest villages in England with a noisy, shuddering boot lid. It might spring open and stay open. Just how bad would that look? No! We need a Mercedes. We need a silver Mercedes to go there!'

He's not up for this conversation. Not up for it at all. Like the last time I tried. I was trying to put him off our icy cold steering wheel. 'I'm sure they're heated in Mercedes' cars.' I told him. I ended up buying him a pair of black leather driving gloves!

No, he's definitely not listening.

'They couldn't design their way out of a paper bag!' he's saying. He shows me the bits. He's holding up something black and cylindrical. He's pointing to broken ends where broken-off bits should be.

'A silver Mercedes, then?' I ask. He looks at me. He's not smiling.

'You can forget that! I'm fixing it!'

Sometimes he's just too clever by half!

He goes down. I'm just not making headway with this one. I need to reduce my cognitive dissonance. I need to fill the gap between what I want and what I won't get. I move on to diamonds. A diamond just in case I lose the other one. I've cheered up! I'm on my favourite auction. I'm scrolling down. This is fun! I'm looking at the prices. He'll be wishing he'd gone for the car. I'm pinged an email. It's that motorbike place again. 'Please pay with paypal. But I don't want to pay with paypal. I've given my details. I've given all my details. They know which card I've used. I don't want to be bossed about by another online store.

I can't be doing with it. I go back to diamonds. I'm looking for something cheaper. A lot cheaper! I brave the listings. I get right down to the bottom and move onto international sellers. I spot some. I spot some from America. Wow! I can hardly believe it! I'm scrolling and reading. Scrolling and reading all things complicated. 'Buyer responsible for all taxes and import duty.' Oh gosh! I don't want to get into trouble. Scary words. I google them in. I can't find anything for people like me. It's all about imports and exports. I return to my favourite auction. I trawl the small print. Oh no! I see something about Pokemon. I see something scary about buying Pokemon in certain circumstances. There are very severe penalties. Oh no! It's definitely not my day! I'm terrified! I've got a santa sack full of the things in all shapes and sizes. All shapes and sizes sitting in the loft. I'm zooming back to my 'Bought' category. I check them out. They're all from the UK. I've been spared. I retain my freedom!

Now I'm wobbling! I'm really wobbling about diamonds! I'm back to the States. I'm emailing some questions. I must get this right. I've already had cause to quiver once in my life. I'll tell you about it.

I've still not reached The Big 40, but I'm hurtling towards it. Faster than is good for me. Anyway I'll lay the blame there. It's a week-day. Nearest and dearest rellies have called in. I'm thinking of lunch. I'm thinking of fish and chips. We all agree. I get in the car. I reach the end of the road. I look across the fields to the hills. It's looking a bit black over there. I look to my right, then turn left. I'm driving along the road towards the shop. It's not far away. I'm in sight of the shop. I'm just coming towards the traffic lights at the crossroads. I can see the chip-shop on the corner. It's busy. It looks full. Suddenly I'm overtaken. Suddenly I'm flagged down. Suddenly I'm quivering. Suddenly I'm face to face with authority.

'Do you know why I've stopped you?' he's asking.

I'm wobbling like a jelly behind the steering wheel. I'm quivering and wobbling so much the words will hardly come out.

'It's because it's started raining and I've only just put my windscreen wipers on,' I plead.

'No! It's because you pulled out of that side road too quickly. Didn't you see me coming?'

I'm promising to be more careful. He gets back into his car and drives off. I want to go home. I want to go home but I'm past the point of no return. I'm past the point of no return and I've got guests. I get to the lights. They are on red. I'm utterly and totally concentrating on my driving. I don't see that all the people in the chip-shop have now pressed their noses to the glass. I don't see them grinning away. No, not until I'm carefully parked and walking towards the door. I've got my head down. I'm going in. This is my local chippy and they know me. I'm going in to a blaze of publicity. The inevitable happens! They're asking the question. 'Why were you stopped? We saw you!' Their amusement is as long as the queue and I'm the last one in it!

Back to today. I'm thinking how important it is to stay on the right side of the law. I can still feel the quivers. I must wait for my email replies before I can even contemplate this diamond. Before I can even mention it to my better-half. I'm pinged two prompt replies. Two succinct, polite, very nice prompt replies from our American cousins. Now that's enough to make a girl sparkle! Never mind the diamonds! I read them more closely. I think I'm going to have to 'Never mind the diamonds' in any case. The legal side of it's all up to me!

I look at my watch. I can hardly believe it! I've wasted another day with so much to do. It's time to introduce the oven to a mouth-watering ready-meal. Well. there's no time to be cooking so near to Christmas! I go down to the fridge. I'm rummaging around all of the shopping. All of this morning's shopping to find this instant delight. It's not anywhere. Nowhere to be seen. Nothing for dinner!

My better-half's been out. He comes in.

'It's OK. It's working now. I've managed to sort it for the moment.'

I congratulate him with disappointed enthusiasm. His black leather driving gloves are sprawled on the table.

'You forgot to take those,' I say.

'Oh I can't be doing with them,' he answers. 'What's for dinner?'

'Well, it looks as though it didn't arrive.'

'Didn't arrive! What do you mean, didn't arrive?'

'It looks like they missed it from the list. I can't find it. They couldn't have sent it.' I try to explain.

He's looking at me. He's looking at me all glammed up in last night's jumper.

'I thought we were up for something special tonight,' he's saying. 'It's no good getting all glammed up and no evening meal! You're just going to have to get fish and chips, aren't you?'

Fish and chips! Driving out for fish and chips in the rain. Oh no! I'm not doing that again! I'm not risking that again! I'm just beginning to feel the onset of that bad mood. That bad mood's coming back. I'm thinking of the garages we didn't get to. The top of the range cars I didn't get to lean against. There's no glimmer of hope on the horizon.

'I didn't get glammed up for you. I've made a new friend. He's gorgeous! He's got dark brown hair and lovely brown eyes.'

'Oh yes! And I suppose he drives a silver Mercedes, too!' He's laughing as he walks towards the door.

'Oh go and buy him a bone!' He says.

I can't help but smile and hug him. He's too clever by half my better-half.

He's gone. Gone for the fish and chips. Gone and left his gloves behind. He doesn't want them. I'm weighing them up. I'm thinking about those dolls. There's at least four pairs of substantial long-legged knickers in those!

In trouble again!

We're up very early. Up very early to get the rest of the Christmas presents into the loft before all our rosy apples arrive. I'm watching my better-half disappearing the ladder into the hatch. I'm watching the smile breaking across his face. I'm watching him return to handsome. It's been some time since I've seen him looking like this.

'All done! At last!' he says. 'Now are you sure you're not going back to 'Spendsomemoremoney.com?'

'No!' I'm reassuring him. 'All finished! All the Christmas shopping's finished now.'

I'm in trouble again! I'm saying 'No' but I'm meaning 'Yes.'

I've been checking the lists. Checking them all. I see they're not even. I'm recalling the sacks. I'm feeling bad. Big apple's tied off at less than a third of the way up. A third of the way up when most of the boxes destined for the rest of the sacks were just too big to go in.

It's not going to do! She'll be feeling left out! No big boxes! I'm back to the list. Only one doll in a car! I really need two! I can see it now. Me? In trouble again! No, I couldn't leave it like that. I'm expecting some parcels. I've been on the scroll! Googling away! I'm oozing success! Such a cooperative store breezed into my life. All half price! Buy two get three! And that's just what I did! A JCB trike! A huge big game! Now wait for it! A doll with more brains than body! A doll intent on keeping warm. A doll wrapped in furs sitting behind the wheel of her sports car keeping warm. I'm breathing a sigh of relief. No making and mending for this one on Christmas Eve!

I fear a huge big box. It's coming today. I'm keeping quiet. I'll have to smuggle it in. Smuggle it in or I'm in trouble again! I'm watching from the rain streaked window. I'm hopping around in case it arrives. I'm looking for a van and I'm thinking about a window cleaner. There's one in the road. I'm thinking of asking him. I'm thinking of not. I'm having a dilemma! I'll tell you later.

I'm still looking out. I can see Rosy apples car parking on the drive. They're coming in ahead of their mummy. Mummy hidden behind lunch boxes. Hidden behind school bags, water bottles, coats and cardigans. She manages to speak. She's got something to tell me if rosy apples will let her. They're excited! So excited! Diving upstairs. Diving downstairs. Leaping around us. This morning they've opened another window on their advent calendars. Big apple's putting me in the picture.

'I got a snowman this morning,' she's saying, pointing to middle apple. 'She's just eaten her chocolate shepherd!'

'Doesn't yours have chocolate, too?' I'm asking.

'Of course it does. All the shapes are made of chocolate!'

I'm getting a 'How could you not know that look?' I'm in trouble again!

'I'm going to be a shepherd.' Littlest apple's wanting us to know.

Rosy apples' mummy's in a hurry. She dumps the lot and squeezes a word in. She's had a phone call. It's presents again! Duplicate presents! Oh no, we've doubled up on Double-D dolls, littlest apple's mummy and me. Another Double-D doll and her freezer will be travelling up. Heading north on its way up to middle apple. I'm flapping about.

'It's OK, she'll change it.' I'm being told.

I'm feeling bad, littlest apple's mummy can do without having to change it before they come up. Because of me! I expect this doll was front of the shop. Front of the shelves in the shop standing right by the door. Standing right by the door just waiting to leap into her basket. With her great big freezer! Oh no! I'm in trouble again!

We're on our way out taking rosy apples to where they all go. They're drawing Christmas into the mist on the windows. Middle apple's drawn me a heart. It reminds me of something. Something I'd rather forget! They're chattering away in the back of the car. It's all about concerts. Babbling away! All fighting for air time.

'I'm going to be a shepherd,' little apple 's telling us again.

'Oh, that's nice!' I say. 'And is mummy making your costume?'

I'm holding my breath. When big apple was little-only-apple she was a shepherd, too. She was a shepherd extolling the virtues of red wine from the tea-towel wrapped round her head!

No answer! Little apple's thinking. I'm thinking too. I'm thinking of yesterday's shopping. I'm thinking I must put those bottles of wine away in case they get knocked over. The silence is broken.

'No! She bought it in the shop.'

'Oh that's nice!' I'm saying. I'm breathing a sigh of relief!

We're on our way back. I'm dreading the van. I'm thinking fast. I'm thinking of ways to keep my better-half away from the front. I'm thinking of windows. I'm thinking of back windows. Back windows needing cleaning! Needing cleaning for Christmas.

'Right, I'm getting on with sorting all the bottles out. That's if I can find them!' My better-half's looking at me.

'Actually I was wondering about the windows. About the windows at the back. It's Christmas! Do you think they need cleaning?' I enquire.

'What's wrong with getting a window cleaner? As it happens there's one in the road,' he replies.

Oh there's plenty wrong with a window cleaner. I'll tell you about it. I'll tell you the story of when I was too young to know better! We'd not long been in our very new house. Our very new house on the edge of the countryside. First to move into the first to be built on the very first row of this newly developing estate. Our very first house move well before The Big 40! That's why I didn't know better! We are gathering neighbours. I'm recommended a window cleaner. He arrives. He's a pleasant guy. He's a pleasant guy but I'm not into window cleaners. Oh, it's not that they don't do a good job, it's more about where you hide whilst they're doing it. I'm dodging around. I'm thinking he's finished. He is! He rings the doorbell.

'Can I leave my ladders on your front lawn whilst I'm having lunch?' He's smiling as he's asking.

I'm saying 'Yes' when I'm meaning 'No'. I'm trying to pay him but he won't take it. He's insisting on 'later' when he's collecting his ladders. Later's eternity! He's smiling away. I'm passing him the money. He's wanting to talk. He's looking around.

'You know people could think we're having an affair if they've seen my ladders on your front lawn like that!'

I nearly die! I can't believe it! I'm totally flummoxed. I'm telling him I'm in a hurry. I'm telling him I must go. I close the door. I'm rushing upstairs. I'm peering round the curtain. I'm feeling though I've just stopped breathing. He's heaving his ladders to the top of his van. He's opening the door. He's getting in. He's driving away. I'm thinking that's it! No more of him! I'm feeling wobbly! Just like Harriet!

We're catching the spindrift on the windows. Week after week we're catching the spindrift on the windows.

'What happened to the chap that used to do them?' My better-half's asking.

I'm shrugging my shoulders.

'I'm sure you could find at least one with all these houses going up?' He's not letting go.

We need a window cleaner and I'm dodging a plasterer. He's round and about correcting the faults. He's just finished working on ours. He's smiling. He's friendly. He's too friendly. Too friendly for me! I'm in trouble again! I'm going like jelly waiting for him to leave the house. Waiting for him to reach the door. I'm thanking him. Waving him off. Closing the door. I'm breathing a sigh of relief! I'm feeling just like Harriet!

My better-half's right. There are loads of window cleaners around. I'm answering the door saying 'Yes' when I really mean 'No!' I'm answering the door to another bucket and sponge. Another set of ladders and two eager faces. I'm breathing a sigh of relief! I don't pay them now. They want it on Thursday. I hide my relief. I hide until they go.

It's Thursday. I'm off with my chicks, we'll be bussing it to school. I'm seeing a van driving towards us. He's slowing down.

He's stopping. Oh no! It's that jovial plasterer.

'What's wrong with your car?' he's asking.

'It's in for repair,' I'm telling him.

'Jump in the van. I'll give you a lift.'

I'm politely refusing. I'm in trouble again! He's smiling and waving. We're catching the bus. He's following us down. I'm on my way back. I'm walking back home. He pulls up his van. He's offering a lift. I politely refuse. He's not smiling and waving as I'm walking away. Oh no! I'm in trouble again! I'm feeling just like Harriet!

We come home from school. We get in the house. Biggest chick's looking out of the window pointing to the newly plastered house at the back.

'Look up there!' she's giggling. 'Look up there, someone's written 'I love you!'

I'm in a flap. I'm in a spin. I'm getting their tea and I'm in a spin. The doorbell rings. I'm paying the window cleaners, in a spin. I close the door just seconds before my better-half comes home from work.

'Have the window cleaners just called here?' he's asking.

'Yes,' I'm telling him. I'm still in a spin. 'I've just paid them. Why?'

'I've just overheard them talking, that's all.'

'Why? What did they say?' I'm asking.

'I wouldn't mind doing the rounds with that one!' My better-half's not looking pleased. My head's in a spin.

'Doing the rounds? Me up a ladder? They've got to be joking!' I say.

'Not quite what they meant!' My better-half's looking out of the back. Looking out to the newly plastered house at the back. He's looking up at the window. The window filled with writing. Oh no! I'm in trouble again! I'm definitely feeling just like Harriet!

Back to today. I'm in the middle of washing. I've left it all to look out of the window. I'm watching a van pulling up. I'm rushing downstairs. I'm opening the door. My better-half's chatting to the van driver. Chatting to the window cleaner. Holding a box the size of a house, chatting to them both. I'm holding my breath. He's walking towards me. This window cleaner's walking towards me. He's smiling away.

'Yes! No probs! Would you like me to start today?' He's still smiling. He smiles and winks as he's walking away. My better-half's coming. He lowers the box. He's not looking pleased. 'Oh no! I'm in trouble again!

'Come here a minute!' he's saying.

I'm following him in. He's plonking the box down in the hall. I'm expecting the worst! We're on our way to the utility and I'm suddenly remembering I've been emptying the tumble dryer. Draping the laundry all over his bottles before folding it up.

'Where else could I put it?' I'm asking. 'You've taken up all of the space!'

'It's not that I'm talking about. The three bottles of red you got yesterday? I can't find them anywhere!'

I'm looking around, then I'm looking across. Looking across to the other side of the sink. I'm looking at a tea-towel draped over wine bottles. I'm reminded of something funny. I'm lifting it off. There's only two! I'm in trouble! Golly gosh! I've paid for three and only picked up two! Buy three get two! I've left one behind! I'm reminded of something definitely not funny. I'm reminded of the box in the hall! Oh no! I'm in trouble again! Just like Harriet! I must escape from my better-half. It's been some time since I've seen him looking like this!

I've got it all wrong again!

I'm making the most of today. I've got a whole day to finish the Christmas cards off. A whole day to get those party invites sorted. A whole day to tie Christmas off. Oh and I've been forgiven! My better-half's come down on the side of justice. He's admitted it! Christmas shopping just isn't his thing! In any case it's fait accompli! It's all done! All over and done with! He's smiling! He's returned to handsome again! Which is surprising since the car's been thoroughly obliging! Playing up again! Oh the boot seems to be behaving itself since its improvised repair but now the car's leaking water. Leaking water onto the drive. I was right! We're destined to have a Mercedes. A silver Mercedes just like Mr. Sanderson's. It's inevitable! Even the garage have sent it back dripping. Well, they're just minute drips, but as the plumber said when he came to mend our minutely dripping radiator. Little drips very soon turn into big drips and big drips turn into floods. I'm sure it's got to be the same for cars. We can't be having the engine ablaze because all the water's dripped out! No! We can't be on fire and dripping water through that very nice village! No! There's no question about it! We'll have to have a new car before we go. My bettter-half's seen sense! We'll need to buy it today! Once we've bought an angel for the top of the tree!

I'm waiting for a phone call from the estate agent. We've been phoned by all the other agents wanting to know if we've clinched a sale. They've got me wondering, now.

'I'd leave well alone,' advises my sensible better-half.

I pretend not to hear. I've got to find out! They're phoning me back. So I'm expecting a call. I'm wondering if I've got it all wrong again!

Expecting a call surrounded by cards, envelopes and paper. I'm getting there, slowly. Slowly because I'm constantly peeking my book. I just can't help it! 'Ne obliviscaris' has just been published! This excellent team have done it again! Oh dear! And again because of me! There's only one story to tell. So I'll tell it! 'Well done arima!' Because I got it all wrong again!

I'm looking out of the window. My better-half's on the way in. I'm leaving my book for the cards.

Just as expected!

'Good grief! haven't you finished them yet? They'll never get there! My better-half declares.

I pretend I haven't heard.

'How's it going with the car?' I'm asking. I'm asking but I don't want to know!

'Oh, it's no good. I'm going to have to look around. We'll go out later.'

I'm trying not to look pleased! My prediction confirmed! I'm bubbling with excitement! My book's been published and a silver Mercedes!

'That's fine, whenever it suits you. Anyway I need an angel for the top of the tree.' I'm trying to sound nonchalant.

'Right! We'll look this afternoon, straight after lunch,' he decides.

I've just supressed a froth of excitement! I'm surrounded by cards and I'm browsing the papers. The car sales sections of both local papers. I've spotted three. All three, silver Mercedes!

I'm back to the cards. I'm thinking of Christmas and a silver Mercedes! Then there's my book. The party! To launch it or not? I'm trying to decide. My mind's on that. I'm making mistakes. Getting it wrong! I'm doubling up. I'm wasting cards. I'm using wrong envelopes. I'm throwing away. I'm misreading postcodes. I'm ditching too much. I'm stopping! I'm getting it all wrong again!

Party invites! Now they're better suiting my mood. I'm bringing them up. Revising the text. Clicking four to the page. It's printing off one! I'm cancelling it all and starting again. At last! Four to the page. Four to the page and it's missing the writing. Just white against blue and pictures of houses. Four! But no invites! I'm back to the beginning, typing it all in again. I'm printing them off. It's working! Oh no it's not! Print one, miss one! I'm cancelling the printing. I'm finding my better-half. We both come upstairs. It's shooting them out! All on its own. It's churning away. Inky black smudges. Smudges of tram lines sitting right across houses! Black, white and blue!

I've gone back to the cards whilst my better-half's fixing it. I'm thinking of Christmas. I'm thinking of phone calls. I'm thinking of buyers. It's happened before! Oh yes! It's been exactly like this before! A different house. A family afternoon buffet. We're relaxing, talking. Talking about where we are at with selling the house.

'Actually we're waiting for a call,' I'm saying.

We're chatting away. I'm looking across. The buffet's almost depleted. There are plates and cutlery dotted around. Rellies are walking about. In and out. The place looks a mess. We're drinking the wine, laughing and chatting. The phone's ringing.

My better-half disappears into the hall. He's answering it.

'That's OK. In half an hour then.'

I just about catch it through the laughter and chatter.

'Those very keen viewers. They want to see it again. In half an hour!' He declares.

'Oh no! You didn't say "Yes"?' I reply. I just can't believe it!

I'm looking around. We've a house full of people! The place is a shambles! I'm begging our guests to take to the greenhouse! With their wine of course! They're all looking irritated. No! I just can't believe it! I'm rushing around and gathering plates. I'm starting to flap. The phone rings again.

'They've changed their minds!' My better-half's telling me.

I sink in despair! I'm back in the lounge delivering the word. Delivering the word to very straight faces. Then lo and behold! I'm spotting very creative relly-in-law crawling out from behind the sofa with his mobile phone in his hand! He's laughing! They're all laughing! I've got it all wrong again!

Just like last Christmas. Only this time it's dinner. Christmas dinner. Dinner for ten and four rosy apples. I'm looking down the table towards very well to do relly-in-law. His face is serious. He's looking so disappointed. He's looking up and down. He's looking sideways and across. Finally he spills it out!

'Where's the turnip? I always have turnip with my Christmas dinner!'

I nearly die. I'm in a panic! In a spin! No turnip! How could I have not thought of that? I'm apologising profusely but he's not conceding. Oh no! I've ruined his Christmas! I've got it all wrong again!

Now back to today. I need a new dress! A dress for the party. Well I got one with ties and I got one without, so now I'm looking for different. I'm scrolling away! I've found something perfect! Just seconds to go! All flouncy and bouncy with three-quarter sleeves. I've got to be quick! Just seconds to go! I bid and I win! Oh I'm so pleased! I'm bringing it up. 'Brand New With Tags'! Just what I wanted! I'm looking at pictures. I'm zooming them in. The sleeves have just vanished! It's speaking of streamers! Streamers from shoulders! They're looking like wings, nothing like sleeves. I need an angel with wings for the top of the tree. No angel me! That's definitely not me! No! Sometimes I remind me of Harriet! It's winging its way and I really don't want it. Oh no! I've got it all wrong again!

Just like the toy for the dog. Well I can't leave it out! We've become friends! Just a big spiky ball with a jingling bell. A must for this huge brown dog! I'm opening the pack. Not sure what I've bought. I just can't believe it! It's that big spiky ball! It's the size of a marble! Oh no! I've got it all wrong again!

Back to the printer. My better-half's fixed it. He's rolling them off. He's over my shoulder clicking the shop. I'm scrolling the basket. I've ordered the turnip. I can't see the turkey. Unavailable! It's reading unavailable! I'm getting told off! I've sent him away. Surely I haven't got it all wrong again!

I've been writing away. Whizzing through cards. I've inserted the invites. I'm now left with a few. Just a few waiting for well-deserved tips. It's bringing back memories! Oh dear!

I was not far away from The Big 40! So, I've every excuse! It's

Christmas Eve and I'm thinking of tips. I'm paying the milk man. I hand him a tenner and I'm paying him £4.99. I'm telling him to keep the change. I'm closing the door. Looking in my purse. The tenner's still there! I've given him a fiver! I've given him the change. All of one penny! I open the door but he's already gone. I'm in a flap! I can't make amends. I want to phone him. My better-half's advising I leave it. Leave it and stop digging! Sometimes I remind me of Harriet!

Now it's the following year and I've hit The Big 40! I'm basking in wisdom! I'm full of resolve. It's Christmas again! I'm paying the milk man £4.99. I give him a tenner. I'm telling him to keep the change. He's smiling away. He's touching his hat. I look in my purse. The twenty pound's gone. Oh no! I've still got the tenner! I've done it again! I'm chasing him down to the end of the path.

'Oh, I'm awfully sorry! You can't keep it all! Not all of that!'

He's rummaging his bag, not looking pleased. I'm taking the change, passing back the fiver. He runs to his milk float without looking back. And do you know? I never see him again after that! Oh no! I've got it all wrong again!'

Back to today. I'm getting glammed up for this silver Mercedes. It's time to go out. But to where? We're well on our way. But I daren't ask the question! It's all getting closer. But I daren't ask the question! We're driving around. But I daren't ask the question! Oh no! We're parking in Halfords. I'm all glammed up and we're parking in Halfords. He's got what he wants. Now we are heading straight back!

We're back in the house just in time for the shop. Just as well as he's early! No silver Mercedes. No Christmas angel. Just a boring old can plonked on the table. My better-half's answering the door. The hall's filling with shopping and I'm rushing upstairs. I'm looking for his card with the tip. The phone's started ringing. There's no time to spare. They're leaving a message whilst I'm searching and searching. I can't find the card so I'm finding a fiver. I'm rushing downstairs. He's smiling and nodding as my better-half's closing the door.

'My word he looked pleased! It was only a fiver,' I say.

'No wonder!' declares my better-half. 'I thought you'd forgotten. I've just given him ten!'

Oh no! I've got it all wrong again!

We're in the kitchen unloading the shopping. A huge big turnip and a turkey the size of a sparrow's appeared.

'It looks like turnip for everyone and not much else!' says my better-half as he's lifting that can of gunge from the table. 'Who eats turnip, anyway?'

'Well it was the one thing I didn't do last year! I'm not going there again!' I'm protesting. He's laughing.

'Didn't you realise he was pulling your leg?'

'No I didn't,' I declare. This charismatic joker's done it again!

No silver Mercedes just a big huge turnip and I'm all glammed up for a bottle of gunge! Oh no! I've got it all wrong again!

I'm back in the hall playing the message. Playing the estate agent's message. 'They're still looking around, I'm afraid.'

There's a ring on the doorbell. Just big apple and her mummy. It's a quick call in. Big apple's eyes are shining! It's nearly Christmas! She's looking up at me, beaming. I hug and kiss her. She opens the bag in her hand. She's giving me something very special.

Something she's just made in school today. She's giving me a Christmas angel!

She's given me insight. She's given me love. In an instant she's just given me the true gifts of Christmas. The gifts of peace and joy. Now I wish them for you.

I've made up my mind. I'll try very hard. Never to get it all so wrong again!

A kiss and a promise!

Happy New Year! Happy new start! And Harriet's got such a story to tell! I've got no choice but to get on with it. But before I do I must tie off the ends for 2009.

Christmas? Good! Brilliant! Well we might have had to struggle round a heaving supermarket and queue for hours just to check out a pack of mixed nuts and one turkey crown to supplement the sparrow that arrived; but we were well, if not inadvertently, compensated by the delivering supermarket. Just one of the army of bursting carrier-bags sat in the hall offered a last minute surprise! No, this was definitely the substitute season for them! Well there's always the option to refuse, but who's got time to even look at the list, never mind exercising the mind as to whether such polarities on the continuum of need are going to fit the bill? We were looking for the middle ground, like a well-balanced see-saw. But no! This sparrow of a turkey was certainly no match for the substitute Christmas pudding of all puddings! Such a lump! I'm reading the label. This is the 'Rolls Royce' of Christmas puddings! Long matured, exploding with fruit! Soaked to excess in Christmas spirit!

'You've certainly gone over the top this year!' My better-half's saying. 'What on earth did you pay for that?'

I'm looking at the list. I see it's been price-matched! It's virtually a freebie! My better-half's smiling! This is definitely his thing! He's weighing it up whilst I'm decanting the nuts into a basket. I'm asking where the nutcrackers went.

'Oh no! Not those things again? No one ever eats them! They

just get tossed. Every year they get tossed! He goes back to reading the label.

'Eighteen months old. Top of the range, this one!' He's smiling.

'Top of the range?' It's ringing a bell! No! I've made up my mind. I'm not even thinking of a silver Mercedes! A top of the range Christmas pudding instead is absolutely fine! I've made a resolution! I'm taking it into the New Year and I'm going to keep it!

It's Christmas Day. No present from my better-half. Just a kiss and a promise. I'm puzzled!

We're wining and dining, almost replete. Just room for pudding. I'm gathering plates. I've stopped feeling puzzled, I'm feeling left out! So I'm thinking 'Silver Mercedes'. I glance at the tree. To that angel at the top of the tree! I feel bad! I've started to weaken! I go back to my resolution. I go back to my better-half in the kitchen battling to remove this huge solid pudding from its bowl.

'Just gently,' I'm saying. 'Here, let me gently ease it away.'

I'm doing gentle and the thing won't budge. I'm changing tactics. I've got it upside down over the plate. I'm banging the top. I'm shaking it and then plop! Half on the plate! Half stuck to the bowl! I'm scraping away. It's gone sticky and gooey! I'm getting told off!

'How on earth am I supposed to light this lot?' My better-half's saying as he's reaching for the brandy bottle.

I pretend I haven't heard. I go back to the table. I'm avoiding the angel. I've changed my mind! A top of the range Christmas pudding is now not absolutely fine! I've abandoned it! That silver Mercedes has definitely weighed in. Tipped that pudding right off my metaphorical see-saw! I've made a decision! Oh! How I've made a decision!

I'm pulling in my chair. I'm missing a fork. I'm watching my better-half steering his way in with the pudding collapsed under leaping blue flames. He serves. I'm passing the cream along. It's back to me. I'm being watched! All eyes on me! I'm lifting my spoon and thinking of Harriet and his silver Mercedes. Oh yes! Harriet got told off too! On Christmas day! I go for the pudding. I press down my spoon but it's harder than diamonds! I'm pressing the middle. Just one last try! Up shoots the spoon just like a see-saw! Off goes the pudding! I'm all splashed with cream. As are near-by guests. Everyone's laughing! Except the angel. And me! I'm feeling bad but in the face of no present I will not let go! No! I refuse to let go of that silver Mercedes!

In any case it's become a must. Since that beautiful village was all snowed up. We went, but not in our car. Oh no! My better-half couldn't risk it! Not driving on black ice and in thick snow. Not with the car pouring water from under. My better-half wouldn't risk it even with his can of gunge in the boot. No! We went along with rosy apples and their mummy and daddy. Our cooperative car stayed put. Stayed put on the drive. Far too much snow for that! We arrived at brave rellies house. Their garden a Christmas card. Rosy apples' very own pantomime in snow. Laughing, shouting, playing. Big apple lying on her back. Mouth open! Catching snowflakes! Wet hair!

We're laughing and chatting, eating and drinking around a crackling fire. Three bright rosy apples come in for a warm. Wet hair! Still laughing and chatting. The stories move on. We're talking of hair. Making mistakes! Hair turning pink! Blonde streaks lifting with caps! Terrible tales! Really not fun for some! I'm thinking of hair on the way home. I'm thinking of my hair. I'm thinking of different as we are sat behind cars slipping and sliding, nose to tail right to the motorway. I'm thinking of blonde. But would I be brave enough? Blonde streaks for our silver Mercedes. Silver Mercedes! Most definitely a must in weather like this. Rosy apples' daddy steering us safely through weather like this and I'm thinking of brave. Brave enough for streaks? I'm feeling bad. He's brave! Driving in weather like this!

Back to today. I'm thinking littlest apple and his mummy and daddy had even more snow than that. Littlest apple's mummy was forced to brave the big hill all the way down. And all the way up to get back home with littlest apple and all the shopping for Christmas. Littlest apple's mummy was lugging potatoes, carrots, sprouts up the hill; as well as all the ingredients for a couple of Nigel Slater's Christmas puddings. She's bringing one with her. One for New Year! My better-half can hardly wait! But I've been warned not to go near it! He can hardly wait for the pudding. I can hardly wait for the party!

We've made a decision! All girls together! we're going to glam up! What to wear? No! most definitely not the dress with wings. I'm feeling like Harriet. Angelus delapsus! One fallen angel! Since I shot that Christmas pudding at the guests. And sprayed streaks of cream into my hair! I'm thinking of streaks again. Blonde for the silver Mercedes. Maybe a few? But then, maybe not! Suppose they turn pink? Or break off with the cap? Oh, I've been tempted before. Especially when The Big 40 sneaked in an odd silver one.

Huh! Who wants those? Not me! It was just a couple. But just a couple too many for me! I'll tell you about it.

I go to the hairdresser. He's nice. Chatty and friendly. He snips and trims, but that's all. That's all he ever does. This day, I arrive in a pelt. I'm going to seek his advice. He's standing in the window behind the counter studying his appointments book. In I go. I smile, say 'Hello'.

'Ah! It's Mrs. Robinson, isn't it?'

Well, I'm nothing if not shocked! I've heard of that old film. It's been out for decades. Just vaguely remember the hype. Something about that woman throwing herself at that poor boy! That poor boy barely out of university! Now I've just hit The Big 40 and I'm suddenly being called 'Mrs. Robinson'. No! I'm not having it! I can't just suddenly become an older woman at 40! And most definitely not one with a penchant for younger men! No! I'm most definitely not pleased. I shall not confide my miniscule streak of silver to him. Today!

I am correcting him. I'm telling him my name. I've been going there for a while. He well knows my name. He's not listening. He's smiling, ushering me towards the chair. He finishes. I can't wait to get away! I rush out taking my minute couple of silver ones with me! I'm into the chemist. I'm buying a bottle. I'm buying a bottle of blonde. I'm getting it home. I'm reading the label. Every last chemical ever created! Too scary for me! It goes in the bin. I find a new hairdresser. I ask for some layers. Some more layers! She's sure to catch those one or two silver ones. I come out with a bob. All the same length! It's awful! She'd got it all wrong! I'm back to the chemist. It looks like mascara but it's just meant for hair. I'm buying a tube with a brush. A brush in a tube full of blonde. I'm reading the label. It's all full of chemicals. I'm lacking in courage. I throw it away. I'm stuck with a bob and my two or three silver ones. I just have to wait while it grows.

It's starting to grow and I can't wait for layers. I'm back with the guy I first used. I'm standing by the counter. He's smiling away.

'I thought it might be you when I took the call. It was when I looked in the diary. You always used to come on the same day as Mrs. Robinson. She's just over there!'

I'm feeling bad and I'm feeling good! All at once! It wasn't my two or three silver ones! It wasn't The Big 40! It was me! He's snipping away. I'm pointing them out.

'Good heavens! They're nothing to worry about. Anyway you've probably got the type of hair that won't go grey.'

Call me Mrs. Robinson! I've just fallen in love with this younger man! This man is the complete antidote to The Big 40! This man knows how to charm a girl! How to charm a girl with knowledge and truth!

Back to today. Still only a kiss and a promise. Just a kiss and a promise so I'm thinking of cars. I'm cleaning up and I'm thinking of cars. I've collected a whole bin-liner of rubbish and I'm thinking of cars. Well, just one car really! I'm resting my rubbish at the end of the sideboard. I'm looking at the basket of nuts. The basket of nuts sitting on top. The basket of nuts untouched! My better-half was right!

'I told you they wouldn't get eaten!' he says.

'Of course they will! We're not half-way through the holiday yet! Anyway the party! What do you think about a few blonde streaks?'

'No, I wouldn't suit them!' He's laughing.

I'm laughing, too. I'm leaning back against the sideboard laughing. I put my hand behind me. I catch the edge of the basket and press down hard. It shoots up like a see-saw, firing the nuts at us both and then into the bag of rubbish propped against the end. My better-half's still laughing.

'You seem intent on sending everything flying this Christmas!' he says.

I look at the angel on the tree.

'Everything flying but us! We'll be as static as her if we don't get a new car!' I reply.

'You're probably right! We'd better start looking,' he suggests.

'A silver Mercedes?' I have to ask the question.

'We'll see,' he says, bending down, collecting stray nuts from the floor. His head's down. He's mumbling into the carpet. Suddenly I can hardly believe what I'm hearing!

'Robinson?' I'm asking. Bad memories this! 'Did I hear you say something about Mrs. Robinson then? Huh! There's no way I want to be sitting next to you in a silver Mercedes if you're calling me Mrs. Robinson. From what I remember I'm never as old as her and you're never as young as he was! Anyway you're older than me! By quite a bit!'

Silence! And I can't leave it there!

'Right that's it! I'm having some blonde streaks! I'm most definitely having some blonde streaks!'

He's on his way up.

'What on earth are you talking about?' He stands, rattling a handful of nuts. 'I said, "Yes, we're going to have to do something about it. I suppose it is all turning a bit Heath-Robinson!" '

I get a kiss and a promise. That's it! I know we've as good as bought a silver Mercedes!

'And no! Don't touch your hair! I like it just the way it is!' My better-half finishes.

We hear the doorbell. I go. I see the postman with a special delivery parcel. He's waving an electronic signature thing at me. He's pressing the buttons. He passes it over.

'Just press ARD and sign your name there,' he's instructing, pointing to the clear rectangular screen at the bottom.

I'm scanning all the buttons. I can't find any that say ARD. He's hopping from one foot to the other.

'Where is it? I can't find it anywhere?' I'm asking. He doesn't answer so I sign it anyway. No signature appears.

'It's because I haven't pressed the ARD button,' I'm telling him, panicking. 'Where is it? I can't see it?'

'No you won't see it unless you press ARD.'

'But that's what I meant. I can't see an ARD button anywhere.' I'm trying to explain.

My better-half's arrived. He's over my shoulder.

'No press very ARD,' insists the postman. 'Write it again and press VERY 'ARD!'

I get it now! I'm trying to say sorry but he grabs his electronic thing while the signature's still there. He's rushing away as my better-half laughs and closes the door.

'You should know how to do 'ARD,' he's saying. 'You've been pressing hard all Christmas!'

'The silver Mercedes you mean?' I'm feeling bad.

'Yes and that too!' he replies. 'Not to mention the Christmas pudding and the nuts under the sideboard! They're all over the place!'

He's holding the package. A kiss and a promise! He's disappearing upstairs.

I'm gathering nuts from under the sideboard. Excited! A kiss and a promise of a silver Mercedes. A kiss and a promise of something else!

I've just read the words. I've just opened the box. I've just fallen in love with this older man. This man is the complete antidote to The Big 40! This handsome man not only knows how to charm a girl with knowledge and truth! This handsome man knows just how to make a girl sparkle! This man has just lifted me sky-high! Higher than the angel at the top of the tree! Sky-high on my metaphorical see-saw! Sky-high into the New Year! I hope it's the same for Harriet!' But when did a kiss and a promise ever come right for her? I must get on with it. I'll let you know!

Down with a bump!

It's The Big Freeze 2010, so no school for rosy apples today. What a start to the new year for the kids! What a start to the new year for the rest of us slipping and sliding our way to wherever.

I'm watching them now. I'm looking out of the window. Just a few brave souls with their shopping bags. Oops! She's just auditioned for "Dancing on Ice". Nearly went flying! I'm trying not to giggle. Well it's not very funny slipping over, is it? I must add that one to my list of New Year resolutions. I'm not doing very well. Not very well at all! Silver Mercedes? New Year resolutions? As you know I broke that one before we even hit the new year! But that's not all! Last night I talked my better-half into three Belgian chocolates. Three Belgian chocolates just to make me feel better! It's comfort treats for me just now. Especially just now! But not only that I also persuaded him to have three chocolate covered shortbreads. Huge big circles of biscuits these! Chocolate on the outside. Chocolate chips on the inside. Again, just to make me feel better! To make me feel better because I'd already had mine! I made him eat them against his will. He's munching away reading the calorie content on the back of the box. And so he should! I've become a poor second to Nigel Slater's Christmas pudding, lately! He can't get enough of it! He's saying it's beautiful and out of this world. He's saying it really does it for him! He's sent me down with a bump! From sky-high to the ground on my metaphorical see-saw! I'm thinking as I'm looking out at the snow.

'Surely we burn off more calories in the cold?' I'm saying.

'We've got the central heating on!' he reminds me. 'We're not exactly running around out there, are we?'

I have to agree. All Christmas we've been marching the scales around trying to get them to weigh less. All Christmas they've been on the up!

They're on the up and I'm on the down! Oh yes! Have I come down to earth with a bump! Party? Brilliant! Brilliant family party! Not quite all the rellies. Brave rellies were off to their rellies. Well-to-do rellies were back home from spending Christmas with littlest apple and his mummy and daddy. Littlest apple and his mummy and daddy together with the Nigel Slater Christmas pudding however, were up with us for the party. The family party!

And that's just what it was, apart from one or two cherished friends. Well that's what comes of dithering about! That's what comes of me subconsciously trying to sabotage the book launch before it ever had a chance! There's definitely a way to do that and I've most certainly found it!

Just choose a day like New Year's Day when everyone's bound to be involved with rellies. If they haven't seen them over Christmas then more likely than not it's going to be New Year! The next thing to do is to make the invitations so vague that people are hardly sure if they're being invited or not! Just tell them to come if they feel like it and certainly tell them they mustn't bother phoning. And the invites you send to the single blokes, just don't mention them bringing a partner. After all, why would you want them to do that? It's your party! This is the best chance you're going to get to have them all to yourself. Well, until the next book launch! And we've just seen what happens to those! Yes just do all of that. Yes!

Do all of that and certainly have it on New Year's Day when party-minded people could well be hung-over from the night before! Even my cardboard celebrity couldn't make it! Didn't my better-half just tidy him away and suddenly couldn't remember where!

Oh, it's not the first time I've got it wrong! So very wrong! Well before The Big 40 this! So no excuse! Saturday evening. Weather like this. Cold! Haven't been out. We're having one of those lazy days. I haven't even tidied up. Evening! My better-half ventures forth for fish and chips. We've just finished them by the fire. Plates on the floor. The doorbell rings. I jump up. I'm gathering the plates and straightening my jumper and smoothing my hair. I'm in the kitchen. Voices! My better-half's letting people in. I panic! He's calling me. I'm greeting dear friends. They're all dressed up with a bottle of wine. They're probably hungry and all dressed up with a bottle of wine. Ours is empty. We're repleat! We both look a mess! My better-half looks blank. I'm feeling terrible!

'Have we got the wrong night?' They're asking.

I'd completely forgotten. I vaguely remember inviting them for dinner. Inviting them for dinner some time ago. I'm apologising profusely. I'm suggesting a takeaway. We want them to stay. They want to go. My better-half closes the door. I'm getting told off! We invite them again. Nothing vague this time! They come and we all laugh. Such good friends deserve better!

How could I have not learnt a lesson? Learnt a lesson on not what to do. Not what to do when having a party. Good friends might have turned up if I'd taken a lesson from that!

Back to today and I'm hiding the chocolates. I'm hiding all the goodies meant to delight guests. Guests that didn't turn up to the party. Didn't turn up because of me! No! All these comfort treats are going in the cupboard in the utility. Minus ten out there last night! Whose going to freeze their way outside there to end up with a set of undesirable love-handles? Not me!

I've put them away and I'm opening the door to the snow-covered garden. I'm looking at the decking running across the back of the house. It's covered in a thin layer of snow. I tap it with my toe. It's freezing! It's freezing but I want to go out. I want to be one with the crystal blue sky. I want to see, but not through glass, the snow falling from the bare black branches, shaken as the birds gather in a squabbling cluster before taking off. I want to watch them flying away and landing again in the garden. I want to see their tiny footprints in the snow. My better-half's thrown them some nuts. But first, just one last chocolate! Calories for comfort! Calories for cold! Only one! Golly gosh! This one's oozing raspberry liqueur through creamy milk chocolate. I'm having such a sensual experience. I'm stepping out. I'm lost to this chocolate. I'm skidding! I'm waving my arms. I'm sliding across the icy deck. I'm slipping and sliding! Oops! My feet have gone from under. I'm having such a heady experience! I'm down! Golly gosh I feel just like Harriet! My better-half's inside opening the patio doors, laughing.

'It's not nice to laugh at people going over on ice!' I'm telling him.

He's helping me up. I'm thinking! I'm thinking today's resolution! I'll remember to keep it! Along with the rest! Now I've been down with a bump!

No thanks!

It's happened! It's finally happened! The car's sitting on the drive in all its splendour with nowhere to go but the scrap yard. Oh, it managed one last enthusiastic spurt in an attempt to sabotage my silver Mercedes and kept it up all day for those poor mechanics in the garage. Just exactly the same as the water leak. Simply refused to perform for these amazingly clever guys. No! It chose to be awkward again. On both occasions it chose to be awkward. Until late yesterday afternoon when it could hold off no longer. Started making horrendous noises for them all. My better-half's wondering. Waiting for the call. The verdict?

'Not safe to drive! It needs a new water pump.' He's telling me.

My heart sinks. I thought it was curtains for this temperamental has-been!

'Anyhow, it's not worth the bother! It's too big a job for them. It would mean getting it towed somewhere to get it fixed.'

Such relief! My better-half's seen the light!

'So it's on the back of the bike for you!' He continues.

'No thanks!' I'm saying, going to jelly at the mere thought, thinking how quickly that light went out!

'You on the back of a bike?' He's laughing. 'What a joke!'

Oh good, he didn't mean it! Now, what better news could there be than this? I return to my work. I'm back with Harriet in his silver Mercedes. Writing away. Getting on with the next book. Gathering excitement about a real silver Mercedes whilst my better-half's slipping and sliding his way down the road to the garage. He's still got to bring it back. I'm phoning rosy apples' mummy telling her the news.

'Are you going to do the showrooms?' she's asking. 'We'll give you a lift at the weekend.'

I'm thinking of lifts. I'm thinking of lifts almost too scary to mention. Well before The Big 40 this one. Well before I'd acquired enough courage to refuse. Enough courage to say, 'No thanks!' Hindsight would have helped, of course! I'm studying away for my OU degree. I like studying away but I don't like the lectures. The evening lectures. Especially as I've not got enough brave genes to drive myself there. Drive myself there in the evening. I feel I must go should I miss something critical. I meet with a friend. A confident friend. We both sit together. Taking notes at the back sitting together. It's drawing to a close. Getting quite late. We get chatting to a very nice guy in front. He's offering us both a lift home. I'm thinking quite fast. It's the bus or a lift. Both friends together getting a lift. It makes it OK. We're sitting in the back chatting away as he's driving along. I'm watching the route. I just hadn't even thought who he might drop off first. Until now! I'm hoping like anything it's going to be me. I'm crossing my fingers as we're talking and chatting. Hoping it's me. Hoping my confident friend will agree.

He's moving away from the college and out of the town. He's asking us where we live. I can feel my heart sinking. He's heading for the countryside roads. It's not looking good. I'm starting to panic. He's well on the route that takes us to hers. He's chatting away asking about work. He's turning to me. Asking the question:

'What about you?'

I'm telling him, 'I don't.'

He's telling us he does! Oh boy! Like how! He most certainly does! I go very quiet as his words fill me with fear.

'I'm the rat catcher for the whole area!'

We're sat in the back, glancing each other, my confident friend and I. Then he starts up again.

'I've got enough rat poison in the boot to annihilate not only the whole of the Borough but the population for miles around!

We're looking at each other in the back of the car. I'm starting to tremble. He could finish off millions! We go very quiet. He keeps on talking. I'm feeling quite sick. We're getting nearer to hers. He'll be dropping her off and taking me home. All the way home down those dark country lanes. All the way home down those dark country lanes all on my own with him. All the way home, just me and him and all that he's spoken of sitting in his boot!

We get to her road. We get to her house. My confident friend's waving goodbye. Waving goodbye as he's closing the door. He's suggested I sit in the front. He's turning it round and I want to get out. She's on her way in and I want to get out! I'm telling him the way and I want to get out! I'm having a struggle to not sound terrified! Not sound as if I want to get out!

He's driving along these dark lonely lanes. Chatting away. I'm nodding my head. Frightened to death. He's asking the way. He drives into the road. He stops at the end, then moves along. He's dropping me off outside our house. I'm being polite. I can scarcely speak. I'm sounding all wobbly. I'm thanking him and thinking I'll never accept a lift from anyone ever again!

Oh but I do! It's a couple of years later, though. It's early morning. I'm on my way to the station. On my way to catching the train to the other side of the water. On my way to college. Going through the tunnel again to get to college. I don't do tunnels, not if I can help it! It takes me lots of deep breaths to get me through tunnels. I'm in a whole year of taking deep breaths to get to this college.

I'm getting in the car wondering about the tunnel. Wondering what's worse? Being stuck on a train or being stuck in a car in the tunnel. I'm being polite whilst the car's gathering speed. It's whizzing along, overtaking cars. Whizzing past buses. I'm being polite whilst it's whizzing past buses. My heart's in my mouth. It feels like a speedway. We're screeching behind them. Slowing right down. Gathering speed. We're racing along. We're coming up to the link road. Propped high on stilts! Shooting past everything. Everything in sight!. Now we're right on the edge. Almost two wheels, skimming the edge of the dull silver barrier, running its course, framing the drop. I daren't look down. We're changing lanes. We're back on the outside. We've shot to the inside. Pelting our way to the start of the tunnel. I'm shaking away. I can barely talk. We're now in the tunnel. We've virtually stopped! Crawling behind cars and lorries and buses. I'm convinced we'll break down! We're going too slow! It will all over-heat and the tunnel will flood as the flames crack the roof. I'm feeling like death as we inch our way out. We whizz up to the flyover. We're back on the edge. I'm looking far down. Down at the city. We're right on the edge of the drop! I'm feeling all floppy, just like a rag-doll. I'm being dropped off at the bottom of the hill. I'm wobbling away in a surge of relief.

I'm being polite, giving my thanks. My legs barely making it to the top of the hill. To the college at the top of the hill. I'm met with a friend. I tell her the story. She opens her bag. Offers me a pill. A tranquilizer! It's sweet of her but I politely refuse. Like I'll politely refuse to accept a lift from anyone ever again!

Back to today and I'm still thinking about lifts. Thinking of the call my confident friend made after that lift.

'Oh you should have got out with me. My better-half could have given you a lift home on the back of his bike!'

That's what she'd said. The back of his motorbike! I'm trying to decide what would be worse. Haring along on the back of a bike or fearing the worst in those very same lanes. Fearing the worst in those very dark lanes all the way home.

I'm thinking of Harriet and her very first lift in that top of the range silver Mercedes. I'm scrolling down garages to find a Mercedes. All those Mercedes' that kept popping up. Kept popping up when the car was obliging! Conspiring away to ensure I would get one. They've all disappeared! I can hardly believe it! No silver Mercedes' in sight! Well there's a few but they're either too old or far too new. I'm watching the smile spread across my better-half's face. He's looking so pleased. He's looking so pleased because he's already decided. It's fait accompli! He's been scrolling away. Come up with a Jag and not even silver!

'We need a car and we need it now!' He's insisting. 'It's this or the back of the bike!'

'No thanks!' I'm saying. 'Anything but that!'

It was all just a dream that silver Mercedes! A flight of fancy along with the rest. I should never have researched it! But how could I not give him one of the best. Nothing but the best for Mr. Sanderson! At least this top of the range, dream of a car, if not on the drive, is still in the story. Which reminds me, I'd better get on. I'd better get on because Harriet wishes she wasn't sitting in his top of the range silver Mercedes right now. I'm just wishing I was!

Reflections

Wet sand shifting
Under webbed feet
Gulls chattering
Squabbling their stories
Flying high, circling low
Life mirrored in shallows
Just brushing the surface

Words
Flying high
Circling low
Lifting the foam
Spreading the froth
Just brushing the surface

Deep water
Still, enigmatic
Life mirrored in depths
Dreams like wet sand shifting
Under webbed feet
Reflections just brushing the surface

Margaret Henderson Smith

Spirit of Thurso

www.ingramcontent.com/pod-product-compliance
Lightning Source LLC
Chambersburg PA
CBHW051055050326
40690CB00006B/722